JOHN BUCHAN
and his world

JANET ADAM SMITH

JOHN BUCHAN
and his world

with 121 illustrations

THAMES AND HUDSON

Since I wrote a full-length biography of John Buchan (published by Rupert Hart-Davis in 1965) some new material has come to light. The archives of Thomas Nelson and Son, with whom Buchan was connected from 1906 to 1929, have been deposited in the library of the University of Edinburgh. Some notebooks and papers which had eluded earlier searches were discovered after the death of John Buchan's widow in 1977, during the clearing-up of her house at Burford. These, now in the National Library of Scotland, include some early notebooks and account-books of Buchan's, and a letter-book containing, among other items, the letter from Lord Milner appointing him to his staff in 1901, and a series of letters from Lord Rosebery. I have made some use of these, in this much shorter book, and I have been allowed to pillage the forthcoming memoirs of Buchan's daughter, Lady Fairfax-Lucy; and to profit, yet again, from the memories, records and photographs of Sir Shuldham Redfern, who was Secretary when Buchan was Governor-General of Canada.

To them, and to the Librarians of the National Library of Scotland and the University of Edinburgh, I give warm thanks and acknowledgment; and for permission to quote from Buchan's writings, and to have the free run of the photographs in the possession of the family, I gratefully acknowledge my debt to the present Lord Tweedsmuir, Lady Fairfax-Lucy, and the Hon. William Buchan.

WHEN HE WAS TWENTY-THREE, John Buchan wrote a poem about a young man like himself standing on the Pentland Hills and looking north and south: north to Edinburgh and Leith and the ships in the Forth making for the open sea; south to fold upon fold of quiet hill and glen:

> *Where the old rhymes and stories fall*
> *In kindly soothing pastoral.*

The young man in the poem wishes to be allowed both: first the life of active worldly bustle, then, at the twilight stage, retreat to 'the happy moorland peace'. All his life John Buchan kept these two wishes: he was always ready to set out on a new enterprise, always drawn back to old peaceful ways.

Certainly from his earliest days he knew both the brisk bustle and the moorland peace. His father was a minister of the Free Church of Scotland: in 1875, when John Buchan was born, he had a church in Perth; next year he was called to one in Pathhead, Fife, where the manse was near the railway, a linoleum factory, a coalpit and a blacking-works; in 1888 came a call to the John Knox Church in Glasgow. This was right in the working-class area, the Gorbals, though the Buchans themselves lived two miles away, in the suburb of Crosshill. John's daily walk to Hutchesons' Grammar School, and later to Glasgow University, took him past tenements, warehouses, factories, an epitome of industrial Scotland. The other, pastoral, Scotland was for the holidays, which were always spent with Mrs Buchan's family on their farm at Broughton, twelve miles up the Tweed from Peebles. Her father, John Masterton, was a sheep-farmer; her husband's father was a lawyer and banker in Peebles; so on both sides John belonged to the country of the Upper Tweed, where fields and woods lead up to the high, bare hills of Tweedsmuir – Dollar Law, Broad Law, the Scrape. At Broughton he and his sister Anna and his younger brothers Willie and Walter made friends in the village (adapting their Fife or Glasgow accents to the local Doric), helped

The Pentlands from the south: the 'kindly soothing pastoral' of Buchan's poem, a cherished Scotland; but on the other side the hills look to Edinburgh, the Firth of Forth, the open sea, and the world beyond Scotland.

7

their uncles on the farm and – particularly in the long summer holidays – fished in the burns, ganged up with the local poachers, explored the hills, and played their games of Bruce and Douglas and Montrose. John Buchan could say, in the words of the hero of his early novel *John Burnet of Barns*, that 'by the time I had come to 16 years I had swum in every pool in Tweed for miles up and down, climbed every hill, fished in every burn'; and when his grandmother died he wrote, 'I have liked Broughton better than any other place in the world.'

It was a happy boyhood, and not any less so because he was a minister's son. The English often suppose that all manse childhoods must have been repressive and gloomy. Certainly the Buchan children were expected to go to church – as were most other children they knew – and in Glasgow the whole family migrated to the church in the Gorbals for the best part of each Sunday, with sandwiches in the intervals between services, Bible class and Sunday school. But at home there was gaiety and liveliness, much spirited acting of Old Testament stories, and the children were allowed their say in the general conversation. 'Never daunton youth' was a favourite word of old Mrs Masterton, the Broughton grandmother; high spirits were not quelled.

Nor was the Rev. John Buchan a stern Victorian paterfamilias. As a minister, he had a mission to bring the Gospel to the poor and

Opposite above: Tweedsmuir, where the upper Tweed runs down from the hills:

Whaur sall I enter the Promised Land,
  Ower the Sutra or doun the Lyne,
Up the side o' the water o' Clyde
  Or cross the muirs at the heid o' Tyne,
Or staucherin' on by Crawfordjohn
  Yont to the glens whaur Tweed rins wee?

Opposite below: The Gorbals, where the Rev. John Buchan was minister of the John Knox Free Church and preached the Gospel at street corners. Buchan walked through this district to school.

Above: Broughton Green. 'The farm stood at the mouth of a shallow glen bounded by high green hills.' On the other side it fronted the Edinburgh-Carlisle road.

9

Buchan's parents: The Rev. John Buchan (1847–1911) and Helen Masterton (1857–1937). 'My father was a true son of Mary; my mother own daughter to Martha. Had she had his character the household must have crashed, and if he had been like her, childhood would have been a less wonderful thing for all of us.'

hopeless of the Gorbals – they heard little from him of hell-fire. He was incurably soft-hearted: given his exact tram-fare by his wife when he went visiting, he would as likely as not come home on foot, having given the return fare to a beggar. As a father he was gentle and dreamy, with a passion for poetry and the penny whistle; his eldest son early developed a protective air towards him. Mrs Buchan, on the other hand, was a bundle of energy, organizing the multifarious social activities of the parish, running a comfortable home on little money, a born manager. She had married at seventeen, and was only eighteen when her eldest son was born. She drove her children on. 'Do what has to be done at once,' she would say, and had nothing but contempt for the casual and inefficient. She was a great reader of the Bible, quick to pick out a comminatory phrase to fit every human lapse; but she had little feeling for poetry, scorned novels, and was in her glory in a good spring-cleaning. She was ambitious for her family, and would talk of them 'getting to the top' – but ambitious within a world she knew. To have her son a minister, her daughter a minister's wife, would spell success: 'a popular preacher, a famous theologian seemed to her the height of human greatness'. She could be sharp and astringent; she could be unreasonably gloomy, brooding on past mischances, plans gone awry, lost opportunities, and foreseeing future calamity with sombre relish. She was never an easy person.

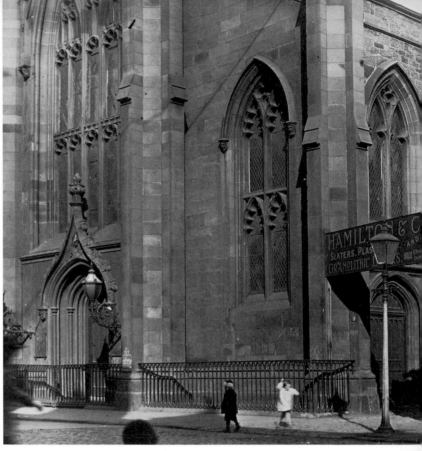

The John Knox Free Church, where the Buchan family spent strenuous Sundays, with Bible classes and Sunday school as well as two church services. In 1943 the congregation united with the Gorbals Church; in 1958 the building was up for sale as 'suitable for storage', and a few years later it was destroyed by fire.

Anna Buchan (who later became a popular novelist under the name of 'O. Douglas') with her youngest brother, Alastair.

The flavour of life in the manse was excellently conveyed in the novel which Anna Buchan wrote years later (under her pseudonym of O. Douglas). *The Setons* is about the family of a Glasgow minister which resembles the Buchans in every way except that there is no minister's wife. To put Mrs Buchan as truthfully into the novel as she put her father, was clearly too difficult a task for Anna; the Rev. James Seton had to be a widower.

John, whose early education had been at the Board School at Pathhead and the burgh school at Kirkcaldy, was enrolled in Glasgow at Hutchesons' Grammar School, in a district hard by the Gorbals. It was a less distinguished establishment than the Glasgow Academy or High School, which served the city's West End families, and it catered for a wider social range: sons of artisans and craftsmen as well as of lawyers and engineers. According to himself, Buchan idled away his schooldays, reading widely for pleasure rather than for marks, but in his last year at Hutchesons' he came under a remarkable teacher of classics, James Cadell – 'There was something Roman in him which made the Latin culture a special favourite' – and worked hard enough to win a bursary to Glasgow University. There, in 1892, at the age of sixteen, he enrolled for the general MA course.

Pathhead in 1870. The small town between Kirkcaldy and Dysart on the Firth of Forth, where the Buchans lived from 1876 to 1888, and where John attended the Board School.

Later, he walked three miles every day to the burgh school at Kirkcaldy.

HONOURS AWARDED—SESSION 1888-89.

PREPARATORY SCHOOL.

SILVER MEDALLIST, - - - - - ALEXANDER FRASER.

HIGHER SCHOOL.

GOLD MEDALLIST, - - - - - WILLIAM BLUE.

SCHOOL BURSARIES AND SCHOLARSHIPS,

With marks gained by each.   Maximum marks, 500.

SCHOOL BURSARIES (Open).

1. LLEWELLYN WILLIAMS,	482	4. { JAMES LIVINGSTONE, - 469
2. JAMES MUIR, - -	475½	{ JAMES WATSON, - 469
3. ALEXANDER M'EWING,	470	6. ALEXANDER FRASER, - 467½

SCHOOL BURSARIES (Foundationers).

1. DUNCAN DENOVAN, - 437½ | 2. JOHN A. S. M'KELLAR, 435
3. WILLIAM SILVER, - 410.

SCHOLARSHIPS (Open).

1. THOMAS MACBRIDE, -	466½	7. JOHN STUART, - - 460½
2. ROBERT B. REID, -	464½	8. JOHN BRASH, - - 459½
3. PERCY HEPBURN, -	462	9. ROBERT BALLANTYNE, 455
4. ROBERT GARDNER, -	461½	10. WILLIAM M'EWAN, - 453½
5. HENRY BROWN, - -	460½	11. JOHN BUCHAN, - - 447½
6. WILLIAM KNOX, -	460¼	11. ROBERT G. ANDERSON, 442

SCHOLARSHIPS (Foundationers).

1. ALEXANDER WATSON, -	408	4. JOHN DUNCAN, - - 340
2. JOSEPH ANDERSON, -	384	5. ALBERT CARMICHAEL, - 302½
3. WILLIAM G. STEVEN, -	353	6. JAMES TWEED, - - 287

Opposite: Page from Hutchesons'
prospectus of 1889, showing the
award to Buchan of an open
scholarship.

Hutchesons' Grammar School,
founded in 1650 by two Glasgow
merchants of that name, in the
district east of the Gorbals.

Some masters and senior boys of
Hutchesons' Grammar School in
1891. The Rector is in the centre;
James Cadell is next to him, second
from the right; John Buchan, aged
15, is second from the right in the
back row. Three of the boys became
ministers of the Kirk.

When Buchan entered Glasgow
University in 1892 Lord Kelvin
(*above*) was nearly 70; a scientist of
international fame, he was still
Professor of Natural Philosophy. The
new star was Gilbert Murray (*right*),
Professor of Greek.

For all its areas of poverty, Glasgow in Buchan's youth was a
thriving and confident city, and the university, in all the neo-Gothic
splendour of its buildings in Kelvingrove Park, was one of its glories.
Lord Kelvin, the physicist, pioneer of the Atlantic cable, and one of
the professors with an international reputation, was the university's
Grand Old Man; but the professor who took most interest in Buchan,
and helped most to shape his life, was still very young. This was
Gilbert Murray, who had been appointed to the chair of Greek when
he was only 23. He found Buchan 'a treasure of a pupil', gave him
extra tutorials, fired him with his own enthusiasm for Sophocles,
Euripides, Ibsen and social reform, and encouraged him to try for an
Oxford scholarship.

'I went to Glasgow young and I left young,' Buchan wrote thirty
years later. 'These were the old days when no-one dreamed of summer
sessions, and winters of savage work alternated with summers of pagan
idleness' – mostly spent with his grandparents at Broughton and his
uncle, Willie Buchan, in the Bank House at Peebles. The idleness was
relative. When he was not walking or fishing or helping on the farm he
was reading enormously – Victor Hugo and Swinburne, Kipling and
Henry James, Ibsen and Descartes, William Morris and Pater – and
setting himself seriously to become a writer.

A notebook which he began to keep in June 1894 shows him bursting with literary energy. It starts with a list of the books he is going to write: three novels (*Sir Quixote of the Moors, John Burnet of Barns, A Lost Lady of Old Years*), collections of essays (*Scholar-Gipsies*) and of short stories (*Grey Weather*), and an anthology of verse about fishing. On the inside cover of the notebook is a tally of pages written; at the other end is proof that his career as an author had already begun, for pasted in it are reviews of a new edition of Bacon's *Essays* 'edited with an introduction by John Buchan', which had just been published. (One of the reviews was admittedly partial, being written by Buchan's university crony Charles Dick and published in the Peebles paper; but there were kind words from farther afield, in the *Westminster Gazette*.)

So already, at nineteen, he had made a start; had drawn up a long-term programme of work (within five years all the books he had planned had been published), and was learning how to market his writing. While his contemporaries with literary aspirations were contributing to the *Glasgow University Magazine*, he was being published, and paid for it, in *Macmillan's* and *The Gentleman's Magazine*, in which most of his early essays appeared.

Tweeddale was where he liked to write, and Tweeddale gave him a great deal of his subject-matter. Most of the essays came straight from

Glasgow University: the buildings designed by Gilbert Scott and begun in 1868 in the grounds of Kelvingrove Park, which had been laid out by Sir Joseph Paxton.

17

Angling in Still Waters.

To some men angling comes as a recreation, to others as a business, and to others as a toil. Some men, notably ~~retired farmers and~~ those who have been arrant poachers in their youth, can be seen sallying out morning after morning at the appointed time, with the usual paraphernalia of the fisherman. They reach the water and begin work. Hour after hour as if their life depended on it, they will whip the stream, and return at night, ~~tired~~ worn out with their exertions only to renew them on the next day. Such men have no thoughts above their catch; if they have made a especially large basket their spirits will be exuberant for a week. Times and reasons are remembered by them only in connection with some piscatorial exploit, and their talk savours strongly of ~~their~~ ~~basket~~ of rod and basket. The last class is ~~still~~ more amusing. There are people who think that it is the right thing to do when they get a holiday, to array themselves in waterproofs, take their stand in the middle of a stream and try an art of which they know nothing. To such men troubles come thick and fast. They usually begin by choosing the wrong fly, and ~~their~~ frantic manner in which their lure splashes down on the water can hardly be

Opposite: 'Angling in Still Waters' – Buchan's first published article, which appeared in *The Gentleman's Magazine* for August 1893.

Barns, on the south bank of the Tweed between Peebles and Broughton, which Buchan made the home of his hero in *John Burnet of Barns* (1898). The Georgian house is of later date than the period of the novel, and John Burnet was supposed to have lived in the old tower nearby.

his own activities on the farm, the river and the hill; they were about shepherds, fishermen and tinkers, about walking the old drove-roads and listening to countryside talk. The novels he was planning were set in his own country; the hero of one lived at Barns, a house that still stands on the Tweed between Peebles and Broughton; the villain of another, the renegade Jacobite Murray, came from Broughton itself. When the short stories were collected in *Grey Weather*, the sub-title was 'Moorland Tales of my Own People'. These benign hills and valleys, and the independent and forthright characters he met among them, gave him happy security and a stimulus to his imagination.

Here is a passage from an essay of 1895, which may serve at once to depict the landscape of Buchan's boyhood, and his rather precious apprenticeship to letters:

The Vale of the Upper Tweed is distinct from the neighbouring dales of Clyde and Annan, and no less from the rich strath into which the Border river enters in its maturer course, in a way which may seem strange to one superficially aware of their proximity. You pass almost at a bound from the fat lands of Dumfries, or the wooded holms of Melrose, to a country of miniature and yet greater beauties. There you have wide vistas and broad streams; here we have vistas, waters, hills, woods, an epitome of landscape, small in the acreage of the surveyor, but large by that curious measurement which is the prerogative of the mind of man. It is indubitably a country of surprises, a dapper arrangement of landscapes which charm by their contrast. The cottar's garden, gay with all seasons' flowers, runs into the heather; reapers ply their trade within hearing of the thrush and the curlew; a meadow of hay is own neighbour to a grim pine-forest; and a sullen stream in one field may be

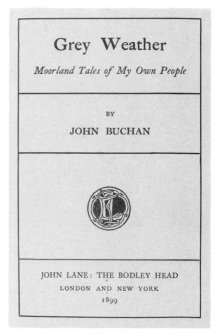

Grey Weather
Moorland Tales of My Own People

BY

JOHN BUCHAN

JOHN LANE : THE BODLEY HEAD
LONDON AND NEW YORK
1899

Grey Weather, a collection of stories and poems, mostly about shepherds and drovers and other moorland characters. Two of the stories were published in *The Yellow Book*.

an eddying torrent in the next. The art of the epigrammatist would be expended in vain in searching for the applicable word. One might call it austere, but for the grace of the woods; barren, but for the fresh green meadows and fruitful gardens; homely, were it not for some great blue shoulder of hill which bars the sky and gives solemnity to the little ridges. It is a country of contradiction, blended into harmony by that subtle Border charm which relates the crags of Moffatdale to the lowlands of Berwick.

This essay, with fifteen others, was published the next year by John Lane, the London publisher to whom Buchan was introduced by his Glasgow friend D. Y. Cameron. The book, called *Scholar-Gipsies*, was issued in Lane's Arcady Library, illustrated with etchings by D. Y. Cameron, and bore on the cover a decoration of a goat-foot Pan piping to three nymphs. It looked very literary, very artistic, but its inspiration came quite as much from earthy Peeblesshire as from imagined Arcadia.

'Everything he put his hand to prospered,' a Glasgow fellow-student wrote of Buchan. 'He had an air of simple and convincing assurance. He believed in himself, not offensively, but with a quiet reserve. His whole manner inspired trust and confidence and respect. He could depend on himself and others felt that they could depend on

Opposite: The Tweed between Lyne and Peebles. During his long summer holidays Buchan enjoyed the countryside to the full, with long days fishing in hill burns and on the Tweed. 'Now is the time for sport, and as the thin rod bends to each throw, and the splash and gurgle of great trout rising strike on our ears, we swear that the world is a good one and life well worth living.' He also helped his three Masterton uncles on the farm at Broughton Green: John (on cart, left), Eben (with ladder), and Jim (right, with stick).

Buchan dedicated this first book of essays to the memory of his grandfather, John Masterton of Broughton Green.

Oxford High Street in the 1890s; 41 High Street, where Buchan lived in his fourth year, is out of the picture to the right.

him too.' Other Glasgow friends noted how, even in these early days, he was husbanding his time and energy, driving himself on. For, happy and successful as Buchan was in his worlds of Glasgow and Broughton, his ambitions (which included ambitions for his brothers and sister) went far beyond them. He knew that if he were to make his mark in a wider world, it must be by his own effort; there was no money behind him, no family influence, or tradition of making career and reputation outside Scotland. When Gilbert Murray helped Buchan on his journey, it was because Buchan had already, at nineteen, proved himself well worth helping.

Buchan arrived at Brasenose College early in October 1895, having won a scholarship there the previous December – a slight, spare young man with a scar on his forehead (the result of a carriage accident when he was five) and a Scottish edge to his voice. Oxford was then a small and easy-going town; what Gerard Manley Hopkins called the 'base and brickish skirt' round the university at the centre stretched not much farther than Magdalen Bridge and Folly Bridge and the railway

station. There were no cars — and as far as the university was officially concerned, no women, although suitably chaperoned girls from Somerville and Lady Margaret Hall could attend lectures. For many undergraduates, in those days of low entrance requirements, it was an extension of their public school, but with fewer rules: three years of games, drinking, larking, male friendships, and enough work 'to satisfy the examiners'.

Buchan's first impressions were not enthusiastic, and he was quick to share them with his friends and family and with the readers of the *Glasgow Herald*, for whom he wrote an article in his first week at Brasenose. He was twenty, he had been three years at Glasgow University, and the other freshmen, straight from school, seemed to him 'a mixture of overgrown schoolboy and would-be man of the world', as he told Gilbert Murray: an immature and rowdy lot, who thought it funny to raid a man's rooms and knock the furniture to pieces. Oxford in general he found too conventional and comfortable, without any of the 'pinching, the scraping for an education, the battling against want and ill-health, which make a Scots college such a

Brasenose College, where Buchan arrived as a scholar in 1895, was then a small college of about 100 undergraduates, with a reputation for sport, hard drinking and disorder. Buchan had been attracted to it because Walter Pater was a Fellow; but Pater died a few months before Buchan went up.

Four close Oxford friends. *Right:* Harold Baker, of New College (with straw boater), and Raymond Asquith, of Balliol; like Buchan, each became President of the Union and won a First in Greats; *below:* Cuthbert Medd, of Balliol, later a Fellow of All Souls, and Tommy Nelson, of University College, who captained Oxford at Rugby football and played for Scotland.

noble nursery of the heroic'. It was like 'some comfortable, latter-day monastery'. But he was soon on good terms with his college contemporaries. With some of the scholars he founded the Ibsen Society as a counterweight to the rowdies; he even tried to row. He made one good Brasenose friend, B. C. Boulter, but it was in other colleges that he found really congenial company. Several of his friends were at Balliol – John Jameson (son of a judge in Edinburgh), Aubrey Herbert and his cousin Bron Herbert, Cuthbert Medd and Raymond Asquith; Herbert Baker and Stair Gillon were at New College, Tommy Nelson at University College. They were a distinguished lot, by undergraduate standards; Tommy Nelson captained the Oxford Rugby XV; Asquith, Medd and Baker collected Firsts and prizes galore; Asquith and Baker were Presidents of the Union. Buchan too was distinguished within Oxford, carrying off the Newdigate Prize (for a poem on the Pilgrim Fathers) and the Stanhope History Prize, becoming President of the Union. But, as at Glasgow, he commanded the respect of his contemporaries by combining these university successes with doings in the world beyond.

His first novel, *Sir Quixote of the Moors*, a romance dedicated to Gilbert Murray, had been published just before he came up. In his first term John Lane, who had already accepted the essays on Border life, invited him to act as literary adviser to the firm. So on Buchan's desk at Brasenose manuscripts for reading and report competed for space with Greek and Latin texts. One of the novels which he recommended Lane to publish was Arnold Bennett's first, *The Man from the North.*

This led to a meeting in June 1896, which Bennett described in his diary:

At John Lane's I met John Buchan, just now principal 'reader' to the Bodley Head. A very young, fair man; charmingly shy; 'varsity' in every tone and gesture. He talks quietly in a feminine, exiguous voice, with the accent of Kensington tempered perhaps by a shadow of a shade of Scotch (or was that my imagination?). Already – he cannot be more than 23 – he is a favourite of publishers, who actually seek after him, and has published one book. He told me that his second novel, a long Scotch romance, was just finished, and that he had practically sold the serial rights. . . . A most modest, retiring man, yet obviously sane and shrewd. Well-disposed, too, and anxious to be just; a man to compel respect; one who 'counts'.

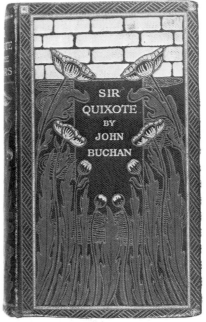

Buchan's first novel, *Sir Quixote of the Moors*, was published in 1895, just before he went up to Oxford; he dedicated it to Gilbert Murray, to whom he expressed his dissatisfaction with both the contents and the cover. 'The binding of the book I think the most awful conceivable – a lurid nightmare.'

Buchan as Librarian of the Oxford Union, 1898: caricature from *The Oxford J.C.R.* of 14 June 1898, with the citation: 'Is fond of climbing many things, Parnassus among others . . . Is an excellent Librarian of the Union. Has been known to catch fish.'

In 1896–97 Buchan had three stories in the *Yellow Book*, stories, poems and articles in *Macmillan's, The Academy, Blackwood's* and the *Glasgow Herald*; and in 1898 his second novel, *John Burnet of Barns*, appeared. His status as Man of Letters was proclaimed by his inclusion in the 1898 *Who's Who* – an unusual accolade for an undergraduate of 23.

Such literary success meant – for this was half a century before grants to students were general – that he could face his college bills with a good heart. He paid his way at Oxford entirely by his scholarships and literary earnings (which had enabled him to save £75 by the time he left Glasgow). He was careful with his money, but did not have to suffer the crippling shortages that have kept many a scholar from fully enjoying Oxford life. His account books show entries for golf-balls and skating, for expenses in Eights Week (a modest 24s) and for club subscriptions, which included, in his last year, a London club, the Devonshire.

The undergraduate reading for Greats and playing his part in the Union, the literary man writing his articles and getting through his manuscripts for Lane – it was a taxing double role. But it did not involve cutting out fun: Harold Baker remembered how Buchan 'was so quick to do these things and then come rioting with us'. The riots recalled were physical and strenuous, great feats of walking and canoeing, roof-climbing and bicycling. (Buchan's machine was hired from William Morris, the future Lord Nuffield, who in a few years was to create an automobile industry that would give Oxford a different look, and a new kind of fame.)

In the Easter vacations there were walking tours with friends in the Borders and Galloway, and in 1898 Buchan discovered the pleasures of rock-climbing, in Glencoe. He could drive himself on physically as well as intellectually, and knew what it was to feel wet, tired and hungry in the hills, with another ridge to cross, another river to ford, miles and hours to go before any chance of food and shelter. Such experiences were to be remembered in his novels, and give strength and reality to the escapes and desperate journeys of his heroes – John Burnet on the Border hills, Richard Hannay on the Galloway moors. Stevenson makes David Balfour, his hero of *Kidnapped*, say of his wearisome flight through the heather: 'I think few that have held a pen were ever really wearied, or they would write of it more strongly.' Buchan knew the weariness, and made it a strength of his stories.

Buchan managed to cram so much into his Oxford terms because he had taught himself so early how to organize his time. Never to the end of his days did he have any capacity for leisurely loafing. And there were the long vacations for concentrated reading for his examinations, and for writing his own books. During his first long vacation, on 26 August 1896 ('being my 21st birthday'), he made out a List of Things to be Done in the next four years. There are four columns, headed

Opposite : Glencoe, where Buchan and his Glasgow and Oxford friend John Edgar walked and climbed in the spring of 1898. Buchan, keen to follow the tracks of Stevenson's David Balfour and Alan Breck in those parts, afterwards wrote an article for *The Academy* on 'The Country of *Kidnapped*'.

BUCHAN, John, undergraduate; *b.* Perth, 26 Aug. 1875; *e. s.* of Rev. John Buchan and Helen, *d.* of John Masterton, Broughton Green, Peeblesshire. *Educ.*: Glasgow University; Brasenose Coll. Oxford. Stanhope Historical Essay, 1897. Scholar of Brasenose, 1895 ; member Middle Temple, 1897. *Publications*: Sir Quixote, 1895 ; Musa Piscatrix, 1896 ; Scholar-Gipsies, 1896 ; Sir Walter Ralegh, 1897 ; John Burnet of Barns, 1898, etc. *Recreations*: golf, cycling, climbing, angling, and most field sports. *Address*: Brasenose College, Oxford. *Club*: Devonshire.

'Attained at a tender age the fame attaching to mention in *Who's Who*,' said *The Oxford J.C.R.* after Buchan had appeared in the 1898 edition.

This caricature by Taffy Boulter of Brasenose illustrated an article in *Isis* of 28 January 1899, in which Buchan was the 'Isis Idol No. CXLVII'. 'He does not like to hear about his own books; he refuses to be classed as a literary man.'

Commentarius Solutus.   List of things to be done in the next 4 years.

August: 26ᵗʰ 1896. (being my 21ˢᵗ birthday)

1ˢᵗ year (1896-97)

Literary	Academic	Prob. Income	Practical
1) Arrange for serial & Book rights of ⨯ John Burnet of Barns.	1) ~~Get a~~ Mods	£200	1) Begin my term at Inn of Court ⨯
2) Write Modern Literature. ⨯	2) Get the Stanhope ⨯	Expenditure	2) Speak much at Union and stand for committee ⨯ at the ~~Librarian~~
3) Begin Lady of the Cause. ⨯	3) Get the ~~Newdigate~~	£200.	3) Take strong interest in Politics. Speak at ~~centre~~, if possible
(4) Prepare Grey Weather. ⨯	⨯ 4) Get College Exhibition		⨯

2ⁿᵈ year (1897-98)

Literary	Academic	Prob. Income	Practical
1) Finish and arrange for serial and ⨯ book rights of Lady of the Cross	⨯ Get the Bridgeman Essay	£200	1). Stand for President of Union. Librarian ⨯
2) Write some of Historical Studies ⨯	⨯ Get the Newdigate	Expenditure	2) Speak & read much on Politics ⨯
(3) Publish Grey Weather	⨯ Get Senior Hulme	£200	

3ʳᵈ year (1898-99)

Literary	Academic	Prob. Income	Practical
1) Write more, finish & publish Historical Studies	1) Get 1ˢᵗ in Literae Humaniores	Prob. Income	1). Speak & read much on Politics
2). Begin my Lady Frejung ⨯	~~2) Get Senior Hulme~~	£380	2). Begin the study of law
3). ~~Collect & publish~~ ~~independent~~ ~~writings.~~		Expenditure	(3) · Stand for President of Union
4) Revise my MSS reading with care ⨯		£200	

4ᵗʰ year (1899-99+1900)

Literary	Academic	Prob. Income	Practical
1) Continue My Lady Frejung	1) Get a Fellowship.	Prob. Income £400	1) Be called to the Bar
2) Do good deal of Journalism.	2) Get English Essay.	Expenditure	2) Work hard for a practice
3) Begin to plan Jacobite History.	3) Possibly stand for Professorship (?) £260.		3) Set of rooms in London
			4) Take much interest in Politics

HONOURS GAINED

AND TO BE GAINED

1893-94 x Bacon's Essays. Edited with Introd. & Notes (Scott Library)

1894-95. x Hulme Exhibition at Brasenose College Oxford (£80 for 5 yrs)

x High prizes in Moral Ph. and Logic classes at Glasgow

x MUSA PISCATRIX selected and prefaced (John Lane)

1895-96. x SCHOLAR-GIPSIES. Essays in the Art of Life (Macmillan & Co)

x NEWDIGATE PRIZE for English Verse (£21)

~~University Professorship at Glasgow~~

1896-97. x Stanhope Historical Essay. (£40)

~~1st class Honours in Classical Mods~~

x JOHN BURNET of BARNS (Macmillan & Co) (John Lane)

1897-98. x SIR QUIXOTE (Macmillan & Co)

1898-99. 1st class Honours in Literae Humaniores.

x Senior Hulme Prize Fellowship at Brasenose College.

x Bridgeman Essay Prize (£20?)

1899-1900 1st class Honours in English Literature.

Graduate B.A. with triple Honours.

Fellowship at Magdalen (?) College.

1900-1901. CHANCELLOR'S English Essay Prize

chancellor's Latin Essay Prize.

Clustered Studies. (Macmillan & Co)

1901-1902 THE BORDERERS. (Macmillan & Co)

PROFESSORSHIP of English Literature in the University of Edinburgh.

As well as his list of Things to be Done (*opposite*), Buchan about the same time drew up a chart of 'Honours Gained and to be Gained'.

Literary, Academic, Probable Income and Practical. The literary projects are much the same as those planned in 1894; the academic include the university prizes he meant to win (which would usefully implement his income); under 'Practical' are his plans to be President of the Union, to be called to the Bar, to 'take strong interest in politics'. Later, he crossed out the items he had not managed to pull off – one of them was 'Get a first in Mods' (the examination, mainly in classical texts, taken in their second year by undergraduates proposing to take Greats in their finals). But these were remarkably few. He set himself

The Buchan family in the summer of 1903. Standing: John (b. 1875), Anna (1877), William (1880), Walter (1883). Sitting: The Rev. John and Mrs Buchan, and Alastair (1894). (Violet, born 1888, died in 1893.)

his targets, and pursued them steadily. 'He seemed to have mapped out his life,' a Glasgow contemporary had already noted, 'and determined what were the things he wished to do, and the order in which they were to be done.'

Buchan never shut off his Oxford life from his family; his letters home were full of his friends and his doings, he had his mother and Anna to stay in Oxford, he was determined that his brother Willie should follow him from Glasgow University to Brasenose. But he was spending less and less time at home and, in his interests, ambitions and friendships, was moving well out of his parents' world. Mrs Buchan, never one to look on the bright side, was less impressed by his success in winning prizes or being President of the Union than worried by his exposure to the alien – and Anglican – South. His cheerful chronicles of Oxford happenings were answered by her chronicles of ill-health. 'When I come home,' he wrote in some exasperation, 'I always find you all robust, but when I am away you always seem to be the prey of numerous diseases. I will be very unhappy if I come home and find you in that dreary complaining temper which exaggerates little things.'

Buchan's four years at Oxford were crowned by a First in Greats (where ancient history and philosophy were added to the classics) but not, to his great chagrin, a Fellowship of All Souls. The List of Things to be Done had envisaged the First in Greats being followed by a First in English the next year, then a fellowship, then 'possibly stand for a professorship' in literature at Edinburgh (that chair was then, and for years later, securely held by George Saintsbury). But by the time he took Greats at the end of his fourth year, he was ready to leave academe.

The next stage was to be London and the Bar, and the plan was to support himself by journalism while working for his Bar exams. An Oxford don had given him an introduction to St Loe Strachey, owner and editor of the *Spectator*, and Buchan was soon regularly contributing leaders, notes and reviews. With this steady income from his writing, he could enjoy London. He lived in the Temple with another bachelor, he dined out and went to plays and dances, he weekended in country-houses. He often went to the Gilbert Murrays, now living in Surrey; and there was a memorable house-party at Panshanger in

St Loe Strachey (1860–1927), editor and proprietor of the *Spectator* from 1898 to 1925. Buchan described him in his editorial chair, 'surrounded by new books, writing articles on foolscap paper in his large illegible hand, breaking off to stride about the floor and think aloud for the benefit of the visitor, overflowing with gossip and quotations, so full of notions that it seemed as if no weekly journal could contain one half of them'.

A.J. Balfour (1848–1930), then Conservative leader in the House of Commons, whom Buchan first met in 1901 at one of the huge weekend parties given by Lord Cowper at Panshanger in Hertfordshire (*opposite*). The house was given a Gothick facelift in 1808; the park was laid out by Humphry Repton.

Hertfordshire with Lord Cowper (uncle of Buchan's Balliol friend Bron Herbert) where his fellow-guests included the Conservative leader Arthur Balfour 'and several of the Cecils'. Buchan's enjoyment of such encounters has often provoked charges of snobbery; but his pleasure in old names and long lineage was rather that of Marcel Proust's hero, romantically inclined to 'put forest glades and gothic belfries' into any historic name, and who saw the aristocracy as the embodiment of history.

One of Buchan's dinners, in March 1901, was with L. S. Amery, lately back from South Africa and at work on a history of the war there for *The Times*. Some months later Amery suggested Buchan's name to Lord Milner, High Commissioner for South Africa. The war was virtually over by this time, though some Boer commandos were still active, and the former Boer republics of Transvaal and the Orange River were now British colonies. Their reconstruction was Milner's chief concern, and he was in England to recruit a staff: the prospects he could offer were not likely to attract first-class men with experience, so he would look for young men of brains, energy and character. He now, in a letter written in his own hand, offered Buchan a two-year appointment:

On holiday in Peeblesshire in 1901.

Opposite: Lord Milner (1854–1925), painted by H.T. Glazebrook in 1901. Milner was a controversial figure all his political life, but in South Africa he won Buchan's wholehearted admiration and loyalty.

A certain sum has been put at my disposal to enable me to provide myself with extra secretarial assistance during the exceptionally heavy work immediately before me. Any men, whose services I may secure, will not be *salaried officials*, or members of the official hierarchy, but will be, individually, working exclusively for me and directly under me. As between themselves they will have no rank or seniority, and I am making an independent arrangement with each of them, the terms of which I should prefer not to have divulged.

I am prepared to pay you £1,200 to secure your whole time for a twelvemonth from the date of your leaving England. You will have to pay your own way out – about £60 *tout compris*. Future arrangements must be made during the twelvemonth. I cannot foresee the shape of the new administration, and you will have to find out what you think of the country and its prospects. The whole thing, as I told you, is a 'gamble' for you. But personally, I believe it is a good chance.

So did Buchan, who accepted by return. Everyone was delighted at this bright prospect except his mother, who thought South Africa much too far away.

South Africa, when Buchan landed at the Cape early in October 1901, was a country of hope and excitement. The war had brought out not only British soldiers but a large contingent of officers' wives, who stayed at Durban and the Cape while the fighting with Boer commandos, under Botha, De Wet and De La Rey, went on up-country. Now, with the end of the war in sight, the liners from home were bringing in prospective settlers, industrialists going back to the Rand, adventurers hoping to make their fortune in gold and diamonds

The Boer General Botha returning in May 1900 from Kliprivier where he fought a successful delaying action. But the tide of war had turned and British troops were shortly to enter Johannesburg and Pretoria.

Cecil Rhodes (1853–1902), painted by G.F. Watts: imperialist and adventurer, after whom Rhodesia is named. 'I don't like him but he is undoubtedly a great man,' was Buchan's first impression in 1902; a later judgment described 'the sense he gave one of huge but crippled power, the reedy voice and the banal words in which he tried to express ideas which represented for him a whole world of incoherent poetry'.

and offering to make Buchan's, distinguished visitors like the Kiplings, who spent their winters in a house lent by Cecil Rhodes, parents come to see the graves of their sons killed in the war. The shame of the early British defeats was in the past; there were new possibilities for the enterprising and energetic. The mood was that of Kipling's 'Settler':

> *Here, where the senseless bullet fell,*
> *And the barren shrapnel burst,*
> *I will plant a tree, I will dig a well*
> *Against the heat and the thirst.*

Buchan, who had not been enthusiastic about the war, believing that the British, on balance, 'were only *just* in the right', was enthusiastic about the reconstruction and entirely in sympathy with Milner's objectives. These were to clear up the mess of war, particularly in the camps for Boer civilians set up by the military where the death-rate from disease was shockingly high; to get the Boer farmers back to their own lands; to start the mines working again, for their output was the base of all economic advance; to bring settlers from Britain into the Transvaal, in the hope that the colony would become predominantly British. These aims were to be pursued in a spirit of conciliation: the Boer, said Milner, was to be 'first beaten, then fairly treated, and not too much worried on his own "plaats" in his own conservative habits'.

The refugee camp at Irene, one of
those established by the Army for
Boer women and children whose
husbands had joined a commando,
and for the destitute, who entered
voluntarily. In 1901 the camps were
handed over to the civilian
administration whose first task was
to cut down the scandalously high
death-rate – 344 per thousand when
Buchan arrived.

Conditions in the camps outraged
opinion in Britain and abroad, as this
cartoon from *L'Assiette au Beurre*
demonstrates. Milner and his aides
referred to them as 'refugee camps';
to others they were more often known
as 'concentration camps'.

Sunnyside, a house belonging to the Rand magnate Friedrich Eckstein which was Milner's residence near Johannesburg: 'a delightful house, like an English country-house, with a beautiful view, and furnished just like a good house at home.'

Opposite:
Johannesburg in 1900. 'The town, but for the dust, is not ill-looking . . . The people are chiefly Scots and Jews.'

Two of Buchan's colleagues on Milner's staff: Gerard Craig-Sellar (*left*) and Hugh Wyndham (*right*). With them and Lord Basil Blackwood, Buchan shared a house near Sunnyside, 'with a view over forty miles of veld to a great range of jagged blue mountains'.

Milner's headquarters were a few miles out of Johannesburg, then a collection of 'tin-roofed shanties, with a few large new jerry buildings humped above them, a number of straggling dusty pines and gums, a bit of bare hillside in the distance, and a few attenuated mine chimneys'. He had established himself in a pleasant large house called Sunnyside, which belonged to a Rand magnate. There Buchan arrived after a three-day train journey from the Cape, and was soon installed in a house near by with three other young men on Milner's staff whom he found most congenial: Hugh Wyndham, Basil Blackwood and Gerard Craig-Sellar. Here, with a Scotch housekeeper, they established an Oxford-in-South-Africa, a haven to which they returned after wrestling with the tasks that Milner set them.

'Milner is a delightful man to work for,' Buchan was soon writing home; but a little later he was reporting that his chief was 'frightfully overworked and worried'. From the first day the young men were given responsibility, and Buchan was plunged into administration at the deep end. By January he was telling Lady Mary Murray (who took a maternal interest in her husband's brilliant protégé) that Milner 'has turned over to me two Government Departments – Land Settlement and the Boer refugee camps'.

The refugee camp on Johannesburg racecourse. By 1902 the death-rate was reduced to 32 per thousand, and a visiting journalist, H.W. Nevinson, could report that 'the pitiful families were now living as decently and healthily as crowds of women and children can live in long rows of tents upon dust and withered grass'.

The camps had been set up by the army for Boer civilians dispossessed of their homes in the fighting: many had come in voluntarily, for the greater safety of their families. The intention was humane; the results were terrible, 'partly owing to the preoccupation of the military with other things, partly to causes inherent in any concentration of people accustomed to live in the sparsely peopled veldt'. Sanitation was primitive, hygiene deplorable: epidemics of measles, typhoid, whooping-cough and scarlet-fever had resulted in a horrifying death-rate of 344 per thousand. Buchan had to see that the camp hospitals got the supplies they needed – there were no mosquito curtains at the first he visited, on Johannesburg racecourse – but he also had to decide on the spot 'irrigation, engineering, medical, culinary and financial problems'. The real improvement started with the arrival of doctors and nurses from the Indian Medical Service, and by April 1902 the death-rate was no higher than outside the camps. Buchan had done his best, but he knew how unfitted he, or any untrained civilian, was for the work. Land settlement, his other responsibility, was far more congenial; his boyhood summers at Broughton had given him a practical knowledge of farmers, land and cattle.

There was desk-work in plenty: Buchan was mainly responsible for the Transvaal Settlers' Ordinance of 1902, which had laid down guidelines for the surveying and allocation of holdings on the unsettled land that was now Crown property. But it was balanced by work in the field: rides over the veldt to prospect new holdings and value farms for sale (with the chance of running into De Wet's commandos to give spice to the outing). Then there was the selection of settlers: many of the soldiers who had fought in South Africa – from New Zealand, Canada and Australia as well as the home country – wanted to stay on and farm. Not all had the experience or temperament required; and there were the drifters and romantics and soldiers of fortune who overestimated the possible gains, and underestimated the hard work, of making the wilderness blossom. By the end of 1902, Buchan was able to report real progress: up at Springbok Flats he found 'things going very well all over the district . . . all our new settlements and our new irrigation'. His hope was that

Some day – and may we all live to see it! – there will be little white homesteads among trees, and country villages and moorland farms; cattle and sheep on a thousand hills where now only the wild birds cry; wayside inns

Buchan the administrator: 'My work is as multifarious as the Army and Navy Stores.'

where the thirsty traveller can find refreshment; and country shows where John Smith and Johannes Smuts will compete amicably for the King's premiums.

It sounds like an ideal Tweeddale or Galloway. But Milner's hope that the John Smiths would outnumber the Johannes Smutses, that settlement would make the Transvaal and Orange River Colony predominantly British, was not realized. Eventually there were only 12,000 British settlers.

For the young men working under Milner* the emphasis was on quick decision and prompt action. 'My experience here is a magnificent education,' Buchan told his brother Willie. 'I have to see that *things get done* as well as make theories. I have much responsibility and I have to learn to deal tactfully and firmly with all sorts and conditions of men. Academic cobwebs get swept away and one becomes sublimely practical.'

Johannesburg did not attract him ('a jumble of contradictions. There are confectioners as fine as Fuller's, splendid shops in which you can get every luxury and never a necessary. The people are chiefly Scots and Jews'), but from the first he had fallen in love with the veldt – the keen air, the sharp colours, the marvellous sunsets, the jagged blue mountains in the distance, like the Coolins. His working journeys, to inspect farms and settlements, took him east to Swaziland – 'long green glens, with a blue mountain at the top, and a fine full stream in the valley bottom' – and west to the tobacco-growing country by the Marico River and the Magiliesberg. (On his Swaziland trip he covered 600 miles, 350 of them on horseback.) On his short holidays he was able to explore further. The journey that stayed most sharply in his memory was to the Wood Bush early in 1903, in company with R. H. Brand, a recent recruit from Oxford to Milner's staff. This was a tableland north of the Drakensberg, 5,000 feet up, a 'soft, rich and fascinating garden land' that struck him as

A rural store in Swaziland – similar to the one established at Umvelos by David Crawfurd in *Prester John*. Buchan trekked in Swaziland with R.H. Brand in the spring of 1903; they inspected new settlements, talked guttural Dutch to Boer farmers, met a number of Scottish farmers and traders, and found the natives 'very peaceable'.

The Wood Bush. 'I have never been in such an earthly paradise in my life ... little wooded knolls with exquisite green valleys between. The whole place looks like a colossal nobleman's park laid out by some famous landscape gardener.' Buchan fell in love with the Wood Bush on his trek early in 1903 and indulged fantasies of building a house there, 'Buchansdorp'.

a kind of celestial Scotland, where the main lines of landscape are Scottish, but when you examine details, you find the water-meadows full of tree-ferns and arums and orchids, and the little copses, which should be hazel or birch, full of trees 200 feet high, and monkey-ladders, and strange ferns, and wild pig, bush-buck and tiger cats. It was a fascinating journey and I project a country seat ... on the edge of the mountains looking down 4,000 feet on the fever plains.

The Wood Bush and the high veldt were the scene of action in *Prester John*, the book for boys that Buchan wrote some years later. The hero's

---

*They came to be collectively known as the Kindergarten; but the name seems to have been coined after Buchan's departure from South Africa in 1903, and many of its members arrived only after he had gone home.

Illustration for a reissue of *Prester John* (1911), showing David Crawfurd pretending to be drunk as Henriques, the villain of the story, and Laputa, the villain-hero, enter the store at Umvelos. *Prester John* (1910) had been serialized in *The Captain* under the title of 'The Black General'.

desperate journeys take him to the places that had most delighted Buchan, and he relived his pleasure as he put them into his adventure story:

Before me . . . there stretched the upper glen, a green cup-shaped hollow with the sides scarred by ravines. There was a high waterfall in one of them which was white as snow against the red rocks . . . The bracken was as thick as on the Pentlands, and there was a multitude of small lovely flowers in the grass. It was like a water-meadow at home, such a place as I had often in boyhood searched for mosscheepers' and corncrakes' eggs. Birds were crying round me as I broke this solitude, and one small buck – a klipspringer – rose from my feet and dashed up one of the gullies. Before me was a steep green wall with the sky blue above it.

When Buchan sailed for home in August 1903, he could count up many gains. He had stretched himself in rewarding work under a first-class administrator ('I have learned so much, know so much better what I can do and I can't do'); he had coped with a variety of problems and a diversity of men; he had met generals and Rand millionaires and politicians – he saw a lot of Joseph Chamberlain, Secretary of State for the Colonies, on his visit in 1903. He had written a substantial survey of the country which would soon be published as *The African Colony*. But perhaps the most lasting of his gains was the stimulus that South Africa gave to his imagination. There was the sense of possibilities, of fresh and hopeful starts; there were the memories of the idyllic Wood Bush, the sinister fever-flats, the green and lonely glens in the blue mountains, the feeling of places where Nature was gracious, and of others oppressive with a sense of evil. These feelings, these memories, were to recur in his later stories of adventure; they were certainly the making of his first novel in a new mode, *Prester John*.

Buchan came back from South Africa in a restless mood. He could have stayed on – attractive offers had been made in journalism and business – but Milner and others whom he consulted thought that if he wanted to make a career at the Bar, he should not delay his return. He hated leaving South Africa.

Any prospect of exclusively indoor work saddens me. I have far too much physical and mental energy to be cooped up . . . A sedentary London life with clubs and parties and books – all that once seemed so attractive – seems to me now rather in the nature of the husks which the swine do eat. I daresay I shall recover perspective when I get home, but I have become thoroughly undomesticated. Marriage and settling-down, even the Highland shooting-box which John Edgar and I used to dream of, seem poor ideas.

Here his confidante was his sister Anna; and he was entirely sympathetic to *her* own occasional restlessness with the life of the Glasgow manse where she was expected to be an unpaid church-worker, always bright and pleasant as a minister's daughter should be, and where she bore the brunt of Mrs Buchan's frequent bouts of low spirits. Buchan did not wish Anna to be 'a blighted being', and he showed his sympathy in practical ways: making her an allowance of £100 a year, giving her a bicycle, taking her on climbing holidays. Buchan's strenuous journeys in South Africa had left him with a physical restlessness, for which rock-climbing was a most congenial outlet, and he soon became a neat and agile performer on the gabbro of Skye and the granite of Chamonix.

Even after Buchan had got back to work at the Bar and with the *Spectator* (St Loe Strachey's guarantee of a minimum £250 a year had influenced his decision to come home), he kept on hoping for an administrative job, of similar scope to his South African one. The best chance seemed to be in Egypt, under Lord Cromer, who was effectively running the country; but in the end nothing came of it. So the freebooting Milner aide, maker of swift decisions, creator of ordinances that affected whole colonies, had now to get down to the humdrum task of preparing Board of Trade and Revenue cases for the Attorney-General. It was not inspiring or dramatic work, it seldom took him into court, often he felt that 'the law is all rather a pother about trifles'. But he had a knack for the intricacies of this branch of the law, and was encouraged by R. B. Haldane, a fellow-Scot and future Lord Chancellor, to write a book on *The Law Relating to the Taxation of Foreign Income* (1905).

This austere publication was a far cry from *Sir Quixote of the Moors*, with its decorative *art-nouveau* covers, or from *Scholar-Gipsies*, with its goat-foot Pan, or from the *Yellow Book*, which had carried three of Buchan's tales. Now, inasmuch as he was thought of as a writer, it was as the author of that valuable survey, *The African Colony*, of *A Lodge in the Wilderness*, a political symposium of which Arthur Balfour thought highly, and of political articles in the *Spectator*. His Oxford reputation as a literary man, very romantic and rather precious, had been eclipsed by his South African record as a promising public man, very active and practical. Hostesses saw him as a young man with a brilliant political future. This was what he hoped himself; but in the days before MPs were paid, young men without private means had to be well established in a profession before they could think of entering the House of Commons.

Working for the *Spectator* kept him in close touch with politics. Though he and his editor favoured different parties – Strachey was a Liberal Unionist, Buchan a Free Trade Conservative – there was much common ground, and little friction; and Strachey made full use

THE LAW

RELATING TO THE

TAXATION OF FOREIGN INCOME.

BY

JOHN BUCHAN, Esq.,
OF THE MIDDLE TEMPLE AND NORTHERN CIRCUIT, BARRISTER-AT-LAW.

WITH PREFACE

BY

THE RIGHT HON. R. B. HALDANE, K.C., M.P.

LONDON
STEVENS AND SONS, LIMITED,
119 & 120, CHANCERY LANE,
Law Publishers.
1905.

Title-page of perhaps the least read of Buchan's books. It aimed to extract the law on the subject from about 150 cases for the benefit of lawyers, businessmen with investments abroad, and foreigners paying tax on British investments.

R. B. Haldane (1856–1928), later Lord Chancellor, as seen by Spy in *Vanity Fair* which, in deference to his philosophical interests, captioned it 'A Hegelian Politician'.

of a contributor so well informed and so ready with his pen. Buchan started by writing three or four short topical comments a week, and two or three leading articles a month; by the end of 1904 the rate had risen to a leader a week and sometimes as many as eleven notes. The leaders were generally on imperial or foreign affairs: 'An Understanding with France', 'The Transvaal Labour Commission', 'The Australian Elections'. The books he reviewed showed a catholic taste: travel, history, poetry, novels, fairy tales. So appreciated was Buchan that in January 1906 Strachey offered him the assistant editorship at £800 a year.

Further political contacts were made through his social life. He dined out a great deal – 'every night for the next three weeks,' he reported in June 1905 – and frankly enjoyed it. 'For a minnow like myself there was the chance of meeting new and agreeable minnows, and the pleasure of gazing with awe up the table where at the hostess's side was some veritable triton.' He was often invited to spend weekends in country houses where, at tea under the cedars, or velvet-jacketed in the smoking-room after the ladies had gone upstairs, he might find himself chatting to one of these tritons: to Arthur Balfour, the Prime Minister, to Lord Lugard, the High Commissioner for Nigeria, to Alfred Lyttelton, the Colonial Secretary. Observing Buchan's penchant for such encounters, a cynical friend warned him that 'if you want to keep up your opinion of your own country, you must sedulously avoid meeting the men who govern it', but Buchan liked feeling at the centre of things, being in the know. This was particularly so in the winter of 1905–6, with Balfour's Conservative government resigning, the Liberal Campbell-Bannerman forming a new administration, and an election in which the Liberals were returned with a majority of nearly 200 over all other parties. Soon afterwards Buchan paid an especially memorable visit to the Perthshire home of a member of the new government, R. B. Haldane, now Secretary of State for War. Fellow-guests were Sir John French, Lord Esher and Sir Ian Hamilton, and the talk was all of Army reorganization and of Haldane's recent talks in Berlin with the German Emperor, and his visit en route to Edward VII in Marienbad.

From the spring of 1905 there was a further attraction for Buchan in country-house weekends: the chance of meeting, at Panshanger, Crabbet Park, Rounton or Tylney, Miss Susan Grosvenor. Her father, Norman Grosvenor, who had died a few years before, when she was sixteen, was a son of Lord Ebury, and through him there were connections with Westminsters and Wellingtons (the Iron Duke was her great-great-uncle); through her mother, born Stuart-Wortley, with Wharncliffes, Lovelaces, Lytteltons and Talbots. There was a vast cousinage, and when Susan went to balls, the chances were that she was related to half the people in the room. Norman Grosvenor had

Moor Park, 'the grandest eighteenth-century mansion in Hertfordshire' (Pevsner), in grounds landscaped by Capability Brown. There Susan Grosvenor spent much of her youth with her paternal grandparents, Lord and Lady Ebury. Moor Park is now a golf club.

been a friend of William Morris, of Burne-Jones, of Charles Booth (for whose survey of the London poor he had helped with research). His wife, as a child, had known Edward Lear, and among her friends were the novelist and artist William de Morgan, Hugh Lane the art-collector, and Leslie Stephen who, in the opinion of his daughter Virginia, had a special feeling for the handsome, widowed Mrs Grosvenor. (*She* found Virginia and Vanessa 'alarming girls'.) After her husband's death she lived quietly with her two daughters in a house round the corner from Grosvenor House in Park Lane; but they used to make long visits to the Palladian mansion of Moor Park, beyond Harrow, where the Ebury family lived, and to the country houses of

The Hon. Norman Grosvenor with his daughters Susan and Margaret.

their kindred and friends. By the time she met John Buchan in 1905, Susan was familiar with Castle Howard, Naworth, Eaton Hall, Ashridge, Ockham, Belton – always preferring the library to the tennis court or the walk to the stables. She knew the pleasantness of great houses – but knew too the irksomeness, at times when there were no congenial fellow-guests, as day followed day in boring routine and the talk was all of trivialities. In London she was freer to follow her own interests. She read widely and seriously, Pascal and H. G. Wells, Bradley on Shakespeare, Hegel and Henry James, Dante (with a crib) and Galsworthy. She was enthusiastic about the Court Theatre, then in its heyday under the Granville-Barker–Vedrenne management. She enjoyed parties and balls, but not as the centre of a girl's existence; and like many thoughtful girls of her day and upbringing, felt dissatisfied with a purely social life. As her cousin and great friend Hilda Lyttelton put it: 'I want to do something better than rush up and down Oxford Street looking for beastly bits of tulle' – to refurbish party dresses for these girls of good family with slender means. Susan knew young women who had managed to make a life of their own – Virginia and Vanessa Stephen, who on their father's death had set up house in Bloomsbury; Ethel Smyth, making her name in music, Elizabeth Robins making hers on the stage; Gertrude Bell, already the experienced traveller. Susan too, with her reading and her work for Mrs Humphry Ward's settlement and the Charity Organisation Society, was trying to create a way of life more satisfying than the diversions of the London season.

Buchan was brought one evening by a friend to dine at Mrs Grosvenor's; and in the polite manner of the period, a day or two later he came to call at tea-time. Mrs Grosvenor was out, but he and Susan had a rather stilted tête-à-tête; he found her haughty, she thought him conceited and difficult to talk to. First impressions were quickly forgotten; soon, when they met at dinner parties or country-house weekends, they were talking away with the greatest of ease. The friendship flourished through 1906, with long talks about books and politics and philosophy when they were together (he was touched by her struggles with Hegel and Plato) and long letters when they were apart; and in November 1906 Buchan proposed and was accepted.

I used to think only of my ambitions, but now everything seems foolish and worthless without you. I think I have always been in love with you since I first saw you, but last Christmas I began to realise how much you had come to mean to me. And then for a long time I was quite hopeless, for I did not think I could ever make you care for me in that way or give you the kind of things you wanted in life . . . I am miserably conscious how unworthy I am of you, for I think the whole world must be in love with your grace and kindness. And I have not very much to offer except chances. But I think I could make

you happy, and one thing I can give you, the most complete devotion and loyalty. You are the only woman I have ever been in love with, and ever shall be in love with.

Susan and John Buchan about the time of their marriage.

Fifty years later Susan could look back on her marriage and say, that for all the ups and downs of family life, its anxieties as well as its delights, 'there was always a glow of happiness about our life together which can never be put out'.

   Disapproval and raised eyebrows might have been expected at the news of this match between an English girl related to half-a-dozen noble families and the son of a Glasgow Free Kirk minister, whose farming uncles spoke broad Scots. Disapproval and tut-tutting there was, but not from the English side. Mrs Grosvenor was delighted. 'I love him dearly,' she wrote to her sister in Australia. 'It is not to say I shall not miss Susie. But joy predominates and I earnestly believe it is extraordinarily good and perfect for her. I don't think you could help loving him. He is so manly and simple and *so* intelligent.' The rest of Susan's family was soon congratulating her warmly on marrying such a brilliant young man.

Mrs John Buchan senior at
Broughton.

Mrs Buchan, though, was not to be easily impressed by her son's
alliance to an English girl who could not boil an egg or sew on a
button. Susan wrote of her mother-in-law long afterwards: 'She hugged
her Scottishness to her like a garment. She had a deep distrust of anything English, thought bishops odd and absurd, and never scrupled
to say sharp things about England . . . In myself she was presented
with a sort of portent: a girl who lived in the world of London and
went to parties, who was English, and whose mother had servants to do
her housework, who belonged to another church.' Escorted by John,
and with no maid to pack and unpack for her, Susan set off in some
trepidation to visit her future in-laws. They were all to meet in Peebles,
where Walter had lately succeeded his uncle in the business at Bank
House. An extra strain on an already delicate situation was caused by
Mrs Buchan's poor state of health. She had recently had some kind of a
breakdown, but would not obey her doctor's orders, and could not be
stopped from working. Desperately thin herself, she was forever
pressing glasses of milk on Susie to make her fatter, which the girl had
no wish to be. But any disapproval emanating from Mrs Buchan was
more than made up for by the friendliness and warmth of the rest of the
family. With Anna – who might well have been jealous of the bride of
her adored John – she was at once at ease. When they went to tea-

parties with the uncles at Broughton Green and Bamflat, Susan could barely understand what they said, still less the topics they talked about – Wee Frees and U.P.s and the *British Weekly* and the strange happenings of 'a cow in a frem'd loaning'; but she could always laugh about it later with Anna. They had the same sense of the comic, the same love of poetry, and they became and remained the closest of friends.

On 15 July 1907 John Buchan and Susan Grosvenor were married at St George's, Hanover Square, the Grosvenors' parish church, by Cosmo Lang, then Bishop of Stepney. Mrs Buchan had two disappointments – that the stiff-necked Church of England had not allowed her husband to take part in the service (that the officiating bishop was a renegade Presbyterian only made this harder to take); and that Mrs Grosvenor had vetoed a wedding photograph, on the grounds that the guests would probably get bored and drift away while the pictures were being taken. People in Scotland, she said, might like to have wedding groups, but she doubted if it was ever done in London. The party was at Upper Grosvenor Street, which had been so lavishly decorated with beech-leaves sent from Ashridge that Susan felt like Birnam Wood come to Dunsinane. It ended bizarrely, with the bride's fond farewell to a strange but beloved parrot, which had to be wrapped in a clean towel so that he should not spoil her going-away dress. Then they were off to Tylney Hall in Hampshire, lent them for the honeymoon by Buchan's old friend Lionel Phillips, the Rand millionaire now retired to the English countryside. After that came the Dolomites, with John enthusiastically instructing Susan in the pleasures of rock-climbing, and Susan deciding she did not at all care for heights; then Venice; then home to their first married quarters, a Gothic villa at the foot of Arthur's Seat, before they settled into their new London home in Hyde Park Square.

The reason for their stay in Edinburgh was that, just before proposing to Susan, Buchan had fixed up a new job at Nelson's, the printing and publishing firm of which his Oxford friend Tommy Nelson was now the head. Buchan was to be their literary adviser, and he was expected to make himself familiar with the firm's big printing works at Parkside. So he had worked in Edinburgh for a few months before the wedding, learning about their new machinery and the new accounting system 'which follows the latest American model and is very complex and very scientific'. This had been introduced by Tommy Nelson's cousin and partner George Brown, a Canadian of vision and energy. From the first, Buchan was happy with the firm – and stayed with it till 1929 – and the two partners gave him his head. He quickly made his mark, with the inauguration of the Nelson Sixpenny Classics, the Nelson Sevenpenny Library of copyright novels, and other reprints. He was also given the editing of a weekly

Parkside, Nelson's printing works on Dalkeith Road, Edinburgh, now demolished.

paper published by Nelson's, the *Scottish Review*, which he soon transformed from a rather parochial affair, much taken up with church matters, into a sort of Scottish *Spectator*.

After his Edinburgh initiation, Buchan worked in Nelson's London office, with monthly visits to Scotland. There, at Parkside, was a splendid machine for the printing and distribution of books, at a speed hardly believable today – sometimes only two months between settling on a title and having the book in the shops; here, in or near London, were most of the authors he wished to include in his list, and the publishers he needed to negotiate with. He saw the reprint series as a great chance to bring books of quality within the reach of a much wider reading public. Gissing, Wells, Conrad, Henry James figured in his series, as well as E. F. Benson, Quiller-Couch, Anthony Hope, W. W. Jacobs, E. C. Bentley (with *Trent's Last Case*) and Erskine Childers (with *The Riddle of the Sands* – 'the best story of adventure published in the last quarter of a century'). He had to cope with some odd problems: Wells was very keen that the reprint of his *Modern Utopia* should be sold in bulk to Boy Scouts; when told it would be far above their heads, he retorted that Boy Scouts were always growing up, and that they would be likely to read a book that had somehow been identified with their movement. Then there was the proposal for turning the *sudd*, the water plant that chokes the upper Nile, into pulp for bleaching paper; and the possibility of publishing in China ('I spent most of yesterday afternoon with Tang-Shaw-yi'). In the matter of reprints from Nelson's French series, Buchan had often to reassure his partners on the morality of his choices. Paul Bourget, he promised, was 'both first-class and quite proper'.

When someone suggested that Buchan's own *Sir Quixote of the Moors* might appear in a Nelson reprint, he was horrified. 'It is a very short book and was written at the age of 17. I don't ever want it

Opposite: Buchan wanted to make the *Scottish Review* the centre of a Scottish school of letters, such as Edinburgh had had a hundred years before. Every week he wrote a London Letter and an article of about 1,200 words; but, selling at a penny, it was not a financial success, and expired at the end of 1908.

THE WEEK IN LITERATURE

SHAKESPEARE AND RALEIGH.*

I.

IT is a pleasant fortune which brings the names of Shakespeare and Raleigh together on the same title-page. The two sum up all the astonishing vigour and romance of the premier epoch in our history, and on the later Raleigh has fallen a corner of the mantle of his great namesake. The Professor of English Literature at Oxford is distinguished from the common herd of critics partly by a superior imaginative insight, but mainly by a certain large and manly common sense. Shakespeare has so long been the hunting-ground of the flunkeys and entomologists of letters that it is good to find a man who treats the greatest of all poets with that mingled candour and reverence which is the only tribute we can pay to supreme genius. The result is a picture, a living, breathing picture, of the man in his works—the only sphere in which he is worth considering. It is the privilege of greatness, Hegel wrote, to lay upon posterity the burden of its interpretation ; but so far as Shakespeare is concerned, posterity has been so anxious to interpret the retired actor-manager that it has occasionally forgotten the poet. It is possible to differ with Professor Raleigh—for, thank Heaven ! Shakespeare leaves room for variety in opinion—but no reader of his book can leave it without having gained a deeper insight into the subtlest and wisest heart that the world has seen.

Perhaps it is the collocation of names, perhaps the way Professor Raleigh interprets the mind of the poet, but the thought of the other Raleigh keeps forcing itself upon one throughout the reading of the book. If we except Bacon, he was the other greatest Elizabethan ; and if his namesake be right, the adventurer was curiously akin to the poet. The central drama of Shakespeare's mind, he says, is the tragedy of the life of imagination.

"He was a lover of clear decisive action, and of the deed done. He knew and condemned the sentiment which fondly nurses itself and is without issue. Yet, on the other hand, the gift of imagination with which he was so richly dowered, the wide, restless, curious searchings of the intelligence and the sympathies—these faculties, strong in him by nature, and strengthened every day by the exercise of his profession, bade fair at times to take sole possession, and to paralyze the will. Then he revolted against himself, and was almost inclined to bless that dark, unfeatured messenger called the angel of this life, 'whose care is lest men see too much at once.' If for the outlook of a god the seer must neglect the opportunities and duties of a man, may not the price paid be too high ? "

Hence one may detect in his plays a preference, a temperamental preference, for those who turn untroubled eyes to the instant need of things. He understands the divided mind—none better. The great portraits in his gallery, which take away our breath by their unearthly understanding, are of the half-hearted—the men like Hamlet and Richard the Second and Macbeth, who see all sides and all arguments, and are the prey of their imaginations. But in his heart of hearts it would seem as if his real devotion were for the objective, forthright type of man—for Hotspur, and Faulconbridge, and King Harry, and Othello, even for such minor people as Barnardine in *Measure for Measure*. His bias, if it be not irreverent to suspect him of bias, is against the idealist and the ascetic, as witness his subtle treatment of Isabella. His true hero, after all, is the "swallower of formulas," the narrow-visioned, iron-nerved man who, like the fellow "of a very stout countenance" whom Christian saw at the Interpreter's House, lays about him vigorously without a thought for the multitude of men in armour. The bias is shown, too, in his portraits of women, who are all of them of a curious directness and simplicity of soul. It is an old preference, evident in all poets and prophets. Their highest praise is for the single-hearted men of deeds, who are untroubled by qualms and hesitations, who smite the enemies of Jehovah so that not a child is left alive in the city. The creature of divided counsels and a quick fancy they understand fully and portray unerringly, but they admire him the less, for he is like themselves.

II.

Sir Walter Raleigh was of the same temperament, though of a different world. In another book † Professor Raleigh has written of the great adventurer :—

"He has the insolent imagination of Marlowe, and the profound melancholy of Donne. 'The mind of man,' he says in the *History of the World*, 'hath two parts, the one always frequented by the entrance of manifold vanities ; the other desolate and overgrown with grass, by which enter our charitable thoughts and divine contemplations.' Both gates of his mind stood open ; worldly hopes and braggart ambitions crowd and jostle through one entrance, but the monitors of death and eternity meet them, and whisper them in the ear. He schemes elaborately, even while he believes that 'the long day of mankind draweth fast towards an evening, and the world's tragedy and time are near at an end.' The irony of human affairs possesses his contemplation ; his thoughts are high and fanciful ; he condescends to action, and fails, as all those fail whose work is done stooping. He is proud, sardonic, and aloof. His own boast is true—' There is none on the face of the earth that I would be fastened unto.' He takes part with others in no movement, and stakes little or nothing on the strength of human ties. The business of men on this earth seems trivial and insignificant against the vast desert of eternity ; and great deeds alone are worth doing, for they, when they perish, add pomp to the triumph of death and oblivion."

No one who has followed minutely the details of Sir Walter's life but will admit the truth of these eloquent words. Few men of more transcendent gifts have ever walked this planet. It is not a case of a mere admiration for the life of deeds ; it is an instinct as swift as fate for their doing. In his Irish wars he showed himself a great soldier ; after Drake he was the greatest sailor ; he voyaged strange seas to far lands, and included them in one vast imperial ambition ; he was an amateur of every art, from courtiership to poetry ; he was a thinker beyond his generation, and a statesman beyond his century ; and to sum up, he knew no more than Drake the meaning of fear. And yet he failed, finally and irrevocably, in all his enterprises, leaving behind him only an example and an ideal. There is tragedy in his death, but not pity, for we feel that he, not fate, had been his undoing. The reason for the catastrophe is that I have quoted. He did his work stooping. The instinct for action and the speculative habit of mind were joined in him in equal degree, and while he did great deeds, he stopped short always of completion. He saw too clearly " the excellent foppery of the world." Superlatively human as he was, there is throughout his career a touch of the inhumane. To Shakespeare the tragedy of the life of the imagination was fought out in the closet, but in Raleigh the stage is the open world, and failure leads to the scaffold. With all his vitality he stops short at the crisis with a smile and a shrug ; he rejoices in living, but without happiness. Shakespeare found his solution in a broader humanity, which, while aware of the dark things of life, sees positive goodness on all hands to redeem them. He had compassion on the multitude, and after *Lear* and *Macbeth* returns to the homeliness and joy of the early comedies, seeing life as he saw it in youth, but from a different altitude. The two worlds had become one, and metaphysics revealed itself as not different in essence from common humanity. For Raleigh there was no such reconciliation. For him the fight must be fought to the end, and the only ¡rest is that ultimate peace " which passes all understanding."

III.

It may be said that such a view is refuted by the existence of the practical mystic, whom Lord Rosebery has called " the most formidable and terrible of all combinations." The greatest men of their hands in history have been the greatest dreamers. Mere swiftness of action will lead nowhere unless there is an overmastering ideal behind it. Cæsar, conquering the earth that he might bind it into a nobler polity ; Mahomet, cleansing the world of idols and preaching a spiritual creed ; Charlemagne, holding the frontiers for Christ against the barbarism of North and East ; Cromwell, seeking "to build Jerusalem in England's green and pleasant land ; " even Napoleon, with his belief in his star, and his perpetual consciousness that he was the instrument of some immortal power—these roadmakers of mankind have all lived the life of the imagination. Yes ; but with a difference. To them there was no dualism, no world of thought and world of deeds ; there was only one world, which their own spirit created. Such men had no instinct for speculation ; they accepted their dreams as they accepted a fact, and fused fact and dream into one irresistible purpose. A Cromwell, for all his weight of intellect, is as simple at heart as the troopers who ride behind him. The practical mystic cannot stand outside himself and see the world as a comedy of errors, and his own soul as of a piece with other blunders. He has no Olympian humour ; and being without it, he is great and happy, just as common men in the same case are happy and trivial. It is a kindly fate which has it so, for the tragedy of the other life is so dark that only the genius of a Shakespeare can pass through it to a brighter country.

JOHN BUCHAN.

* *Shakespeare.* By Walter Raleigh. "English Men of Letters." Macmillan and Co.

† *The English Voyagers of the Sixteenth Century* (p. 110).

Buchan with his daughter Alice, born in 1908.

republished.' But he was ready to write new books for Nelson's. The first two were boys' books. One was the life of Sir Walter Raleigh, told in eleven stories: 'it is crammed full of really accurate history, though I have endeavoured to make it as much like fiction as possible.' The other was *Prester John*, the tale of a lad from Fife who goes to seek his fortune in the Transvaal, into which Buchan could put his own exhilaration about riding on the veldt, penetrating the Wood Bush, catching hints of old mysteries. His third book for Nelson's was the life of the Marquis of Montrose, one of his heroes since boyhood.

By the standards of the time, the Buchans were well off for a young couple, and they had the luck to live at a time when houses in central London could be rented for £250 a year. So after their first child Alice was born (in 1908) they moved from Hyde Park Square to 13 Bryanston Street; and after Johnnie's birth (in 1911) they moved again, to 76 Portland Place – a charming Adam-style house near the Regent's Park end with garlanded mantelpieces and pretty cornices ('I have given £500 for the landlord to do the rebuilding, hot-water, drainage etc'). Buchan was to put his knowledge of the ins and outs of

Portland Place, to which the Buchans moved in 1912 – and where Richard Hannay's adventures started in 1914. Their house, number 76, at the far end, had some elegant ceilings and cornices.

Marylebone to good use in *The Power-House* ('a tribute at the shrine of my master in fiction – E. Phillips Oppenheim') and in *The Three Hostages*, where the sinister nightclub The Fields of Eden is situated in one of the streets near Fitzroy Square.

The Buchans were much in demand as guests at dinner-parties and country-house weekends. They were often with Susan's widowed aunt, Lady Lovelace, at her Surrey home at Ockham (a house described in William de Morgan's novel, *Joseph Vance*), or at the romantic Ashley Combe, near Porlock. Buchan would be asked to play host at the dinner-table – and had one highly embarrassing moment when, having pressed Henry James to take some very special old Madeira, he discovered on tasting it himself that it was some vile liquor substituted by a dishonest butler.

In the spring of 1910 they travelled by the Orient Express to Constantinople, where they joined Buchan's colleague of South African days, Gerard Craig-Sellar, on his yacht *Rannoch*. The meeting lacked the excitement of Hannay's rendezvous in that city with Sandy Arbuthnot and the Companions of the Rosy Hours, but some poking round the bazaars, and discussions with some of the Young Turks, left vivid impressions which were to give authenticity and colour to the latter part of *Greenmantle*. More impressions were harvested for future use as they cruised in the Aegean: in particular, the sight of a shuttered house in a walled garden by the landing-stage of one of the Petali islands, which became the germ of *The Dancing Floor*. In 1911 they stayed with Moritz Bonn – a young German economist who had come to teach at the London School of Economics – in Bavaria, at midsummer, when the bonfires were lit and the young men of the village jumped through them. The next spring they were in Norway with Tommy Nelson, fishing the Leardal.

Other holidays were spent in Peeblesshire, to which Buchan was drawn now by more than old affection and family ties. In 1911 he was adopted as Unionist candidate for Peeblesshire and Selkirk. Choice of a party was for him more a matter of tone than of dogma. He had many Liberal friends – Gilbert Murray, Raymond Asquith, R. B. Haldane – and shared many of their views, especially on free trade and the need for old-age and unemployment insurance. But in Scotland the Liberals were the established party (the Unionists had collected only 11 seats in the 1906 election) and to Buchan they showed the weaknesses of establishment: rigidity, complacency and unctuousness. Their dogmas, he said,

were so completely taken for granted that their presentation partook less of argument than of a tribal incantation. Mr Gladstone had given it an aura of earnest morality, so that its platforms were also pulpits and its harangues had the weight of sermons.

Yet, although standing as a Unionist, he felt it quite in order to invite a distinguished former Liberal to take the chair at one of his meetings: this was Lord Rosebery, Prime Minister in 1894–5, and now withdrawn from politics. Rosebery firmly refused (though had he been in Scotland, he said, he would have sat in the audience 'in a domino'), but warmly invited Buchan to visit him at his house in the Moorfoot Hills when 'stumping your harassed Peeblesshire'. So began a friendship that lasted until Rosebery's death in 1929.

Indeed, as Buchan's close friends realized, he was no perfervid party man. His Tory friend L. S. Amery, his Liberal friend Charles Masterman (a member of the Liberal administration and a cousin of Susan's by marriage) had both begged him to declare himself. 'Don't let him be a mugwump,' Masterman told Susan, 'let him join either the Liberals or the Tories, I don't mind which.' After his adoption meeting, the *Peebles News* wondered: 'Is the Candidate a Liberal?'

Mr John Buchan is rather advanced in his opinions to please some of the more rabid Tories. Part of his programme is stated to be: Abolition of the hereditary principle of the House of Lords, Free Trade, and a scheme of Small Holdings. How the Unionist Tariff Reformers will act with such a programme remains to be seen. Certain it is that some who attended the meeting are not at all keen on such an advanced programme.

Left: Charles Masterman (1873–1924) was Liberal MP for West Ham, and under-secretary in the Asquith administration, in the Cabinet 1914–1915 and then Director of War Propaganda. He married Susan Buchan's cousin, Lucy Lyttelton.

Lord Rosebery (1847–1929), as seen by Harry Furniss. Prime Minister 1894–95, and leader of the Liberal Party, he retired from active politics in 1905. He had three houses in Scotland and three in England (including Mentmore), he married an heiress, won the Derby three times, and wrote lives of Pitt and Napoleon. Buchan was fascinated by Rosebery's combination of gifts, by his style, and by the duality 'of the polished eighteenth-century grandee who loved the apparatus of life, and the seventeenth-century Scottish Calvinist who saw only its triviality'.

Loch, hill and moor in Ross-shire — Buchan spent many holidays in the Western Highlands, fishing, stalking and climbing, and that country was to give him the background for *John Macnab* and the climax of *The Three Hostages*.

He was still a convinced Imperialist, but he no longer followed Milner in his hopes of an Imperial Federation, and was never a member of the Round Table, a group inspired by that idea.

I realised what Sir Wilfred Laurier, first of all imperial statesmen, realised, that you could not bind a growing Empire with any elaborate constitutional bonds. I realised the strength of Colonial nationalism — that the different Dominions had still to rise to national stature, and that until that day came, it was idle to talk about any machinery of union.

Buchan enjoyed nursing his constituency, for it took him back to the world of his boyhood: his kind of electioneering allowed for long walks up the glens of Tweed, Ettrick and Yarrow, and long talks with farmers, shepherds and anglers, not by any means confined to politics. Once at a lamb-fair a shepherd paid him a compliment he relished: 'Your predecessor was an awfu' nice man, but he was far ower much of a gentleman and far ower honest.' But as well as these happily-remembered days there were the trials suffered by anybody who woos a scattered rural constituency far from his own home: meetings in draughty halls after nothing more sustaining than a meat pie and a cup of tea; waiting for train connections in chilly stations; listening to the same well-worn songs and recitations at the 'entertainment' after the political business.

Every time he came north, to Peeblesshire or Edinburgh, he tried to see his parents. These were not good years for the senior Buchans. Mr Buchan had been persuaded to retire from his church in 1910 (John and his brother William supplementing his meagre pension) and they had settled in Peebles, not far from Walter and Anna at the Bank House. Then Mrs Buchan was gravely ill; as she recovered, her husband died, worn out with his hard work in the Gorbals; and in 1912 William Buchan, home on leave from India, contracted a mysterious disease and died too. Buchan felt this very sorely, for they had been close friends as well as brothers, and he had taken great pride in William's career at Brasenose and in the Indian Civil Service. 'We will never get over this,' he told Susan. Increasingly, the burden of his mother's depressions fell on him: her letters − which arrived almost daily, and to which she expected immediate replies − were full of complaints and apprehensions. She went into perpetual mourning when her husband died; she seemed to relish gloom.

Such pressures, in his public and personal life, made their mark on Buchan's health. In 1912 he began to be troubled with attacks which were first labelled indigestion, then diagnosed as a duodenal ulcer: an enemy that was to dog him for the rest of his life. In July 1914 Susan was very anxious about him, and about their daughter Alice who had just been severely ill with mastoid. Sea air was ordered, and Susan and

Bank House, Peebles, the corner house where the law and banking business established by Buchan's paternal grandfather was carried on by his uncle Willie. When Buchan's brother Walter succeeded his uncle in 1906 as Town Clerk of Peebles, he brought his sister Anna to live with him at Bank House, and after the Rev. John Buchan's death, his mother lived there too. It remained a Buchan home till Walter's death in 1954.

the children went off to Broadstairs; Buchan stayed on in London for a day or two (breakfasting with Sir Edward Grey, the Foreign Secretary, two days before the declaration of war on Germany), then joined them at their lodgings. Susan's cousins, Arthur and Hilda Grenfell, were not far away, in a house with steps down to the beach. Doctor's orders were to rest, in bed; Buchan obeyed, but his mind galloped on. He was concerned with the effect of the war on Nelson's, and the likely collapse of the Continental business, and hoped that the printing-works could be kept going at least at half-power, so as not to throw too many out of work. By 14 August he had come up with the idea of publishing a history of the war in monthly parts with, he suggested, Hilaire Belloc as author. His colleagues in Edinburgh agreed at once; but Belloc was not available, and in the end it was Buchan himself who took it on. By mid-October he had written the first part, and was also midway in a 'shocker' which he dedicated to Tommy Nelson: *The Thirty-Nine Steps*.

Work on the Nelson *History* soon made Buchan an authority on the progress of the war, though he would much rather have been a combatant – like Tommy Nelson in the Lothian and Border Horse, Raymond Asquith in the Queens' Westminsters, his younger brother Alastair in the Cameron Highlanders, and short-sighted Aubrey Herbert, who had brazened himself into the Irish Guards simply by joining a detachment marching down Birdcage Walk on their way to the troop train. Buchan's health ruled out an active soldier's role, but in

Opposite:
The moors of Galloway, where Richard Hannay, in *The Thirty-Nine Steps*, was relentlessly hunted from the ground and from the air. 'The aeroplane was flying high, but as I looked it dropped several hundred feet and began to circle round the knot of hill in narrowing circles, just as a hawk wheels before it pounces.'

A long way from *The Thirty-Nine Steps*: the climax of the third (1978) film version, with the hero (played by Robert Powell) acting more like Harold Lloyd than Richard Hannay in a desperate effort to stop the hand of Big Ben, an episode not in the book. Hitchcock directed the first *Thirty-Nine Steps* film in 1935 with Robert Donat as Hannay; the second (1958) had Kenneth More.

Dedication of *The Thirty-Nine Steps* (1915).

Buchan in uniform as a lieutenant-colonel in the Intelligence Corps, with his son Johnnie and his brother Alastair, Royal Scots Fusiliers, who died of wounds after the battle of Arras in the spring of 1917.

the next four years he was to see more of the war, with the fighting men in France and Flanders and with the politicians at home, than he could have dreamed of during the dismal days at Broadstairs when he wrote *The Thirty-Nine Steps* to take his mind off his ulcer.

The *History* which, to begin with, appeared in fortnightly parts, and a series of successful public lectures on the course of the war, led to Buchan's being invited by *The Times* to visit the Front as its special correspondent. So in May 1915 he was in Flanders; the five articles he wrote appeared under his own name (unusual in *The Times* of that day) and made an effective contrast to the official communiqués with their impersonal reports: 'The enemy made several attacks between the sea and Arras. Our infantry threw them back, inflicting heavy losses.' Buchan wanted to explain the military situation to the reader at home, but also to give him some idea of the feel and character of this war which brought British soldiers to Western Europe for the first time in a hundred years. 'Battles in this war are not pictures for the eye. They are assaults on the ear.'

The first article was entitled 'On a Flemish Hill' and began:

It is only a little hill, but in this flat country it is a viewpoint to be thankful for. A round knuckle of green 100 feet or so above the plain, it commands almost the whole extent of the British front. Behind are the ridges which march by the Mont des Cats and the Hill of Cassel to the uplands behind St Omer. North are the low levels towards Dixmude, and south the valley of the Lys and the plains towards the Scarpe and the Scheldt. In front, a few miles off, are the trench lines round which has been waged one of the greatest battles in the world.

This was the second battle of Ypres, on ground, Buchan reminded his readers, that had been fought over for 2,000 years.

In the winter it was a bleak landscape, with stagnant water in every bottom and draggled woods of larch and water-logged meadows. Now, in this second week of May, it is green as Oxfordshire. This morning it rained, and the wind blew from the north. The wind still blows, but the rain has gone, and white clouds drift in a clear sky, as in some Flemish painting. Here, on the hillside, broom and lilac and wild hyacinths are everywhere. Cattle graze in fields round the little red homesteads below, and for a moment, a man might delude himself with the belief that he was looking on some prosperous spring champaign in the happy days of peace. But there are sights and sounds that break the illusion.

He went on to describe the puffs of smoke, the muffled booming, the zigzag scars of trenches on the hills, that spoke of the present grim reality. He wanted the reader to see what the places made familiar in the communiqués were really like – Ploegsteert Wood; Hill 60, 'that brownish patch to the right of the distant church-spire'; Ypres with the skeletons of the Church of St Martin and the Cloth Hall.

The ruins of Ypres, showing St Martin's Cathedral.

British troops moving up the Menin road to the east of Ypres.

One day he was allowed into that city, and noted how 'Civil life goes on up to the very edge of the fire zone. In the hamlets girls sit outside their doors busy at lacemaking; the country people are at work in the fields, and children are playing round the cottages' — but one step further, and it was like being in Pompeii. He noticed the detail in the silent ruins — 'a painstaking starling is rebuilding its nest in a broken pinnacle. An old cow, a miserable object, is poking her head in the debris and sniffing anxiously at the dead body of a horse.'

In other articles he wrote about the troops. He visited the Argyll and Sutherland Highlanders and talked with 'mechanics from the cities and tradesmen from the towns and ploughmen from the Carse of Stirling and herds from the Ochils'; he praised the Territorials from Northumberland and Durham, 'one of the finest fighting stocks on earth . . . led by officers who a year ago had been architects and solicitors and businessmen.'

Throughout his articles he stressed the German superiority in armament (this was a time of acute shell shortage on the British front) — 'we must master his artillery before we fling our infantry at him' — and while praising the British soldier, he reminded his readers that 'the enemy is skilled and obstinate and incredibly brave'. One of the German generals he mentioned (*Greenmantle* fans may like to know) was General von Einem.

Douglas Haig was one of the British generals whom Buchan met at General Headquarters, and it was probably at Haig's request that the War Office asked Buchan to go out again in September to report on the battle of Loos. This time he was in uniform as a lieutenant (soon to be major, then colonel) in the Intelligence Corps; and the address he gave his wife (staying with her in-laws at Peebles) was GHQ, BEF. He was out for just under a fortnight, during which the early hopes — 'We are doing splendidly . . . The Hun is at last being firmly handled' — faded as the casualties mounted. 'I fear we have paid a big price for success.'

The Foreign Office too was keen to use him; and in February 1916 he was asked to take a Russian delegation to Scapa Flow:

I am off to the Grand Fleet tonight with the Russians. The Pentland Firth is a queasy waterway. The Government are doing us very comfortably, giving us a special train with a restaurant car. We had a tremendous week of festivities for the Russians last week, which went off very well, though I am pretty well sick of them.

One of the delegates, Protopopov (who a year later was to throw in his lot with the Tsarina and Rasputin), slept so badly in his hotel that Buchan invited him to stay: he startled his host by his energetic recital of 'A Frog he would a-wooing go' and other nursery rhymes learnt from his English nanny.

By June, Buchan was regularly employed by the Foreign Office on intelligence, and directly responsible to the Foreign Secretary, Sir Edward Grey; he was also attached to Haig's staff in France, and made six further visits to GHQ in 1916. It was hard going, and he saw no prospect of a holiday 'till the end of this bloody war'; at the same time, it was 'the most interesting job on the globe for I live at the heart of things here and in France'. He was always reassuring Susan that in his office at GHQ, in his billet with 'a queer old French lady who is always inviting me to come to her kitchen fire', he was running no risk, and was leading 'a life of most inglorious security'. But looking back many years later he called this time in France 'purgatorial',

for though I had few of the hardships of the actual trenches, lengthy journeys in the drizzling autumn and winter of 1916, damp billets, and irregular meals reduced me to such a state of physical wretchedness that even today a kind of nausea seizes me when some smell recalls the festering odour of the front line, made up of incinerators, latrines and mud.

His ulcer gave him some very bad days, and he was often reduced to a dull diet of Allenbury's and Benger's, bland invalid food. He passed on his ulcer to his fictional creature Blenkiron, who made his first appearance that autumn in *Greenmantle*; and like Blenkiron (in the later *Mr Standfast*), Buchan underwent the short-circuit operation early in 1917, though the results were not so happy in fact as they were in fiction. This may well have been because Buchan allowed himself no proper convalescence; he was itching to be up and doing in yet another new job.

This was a by-product of the political upheaval of December 1916, when Lloyd George replaced Asquith as Prime Minister and formed a small War Cabinet, which included Milner. One of the Cabinet's early objectives was to improve propaganda, and Buchan was asked to prepare a memorandum with proposals for a new Department of Information. His proposals were approved and, by a Cabinet minute, the department was set up with Buchan (strongly backed by Milner) as its first director, responsible directly to the Prime Minister. Later in 1917 the department became a ministry, when Buchan worked first under the Ulster politician Edward Carson then (and much more happily) under Beaverbrook.

The world he now moved in comprised his own department (whose separate sections were inconveniently scattered round the Strand), the Foreign Office, Admiralty, War Office, No. 10 Downing Street and – occasionally – Buckingham Palace. The work was varied and strenuous, but Buchan was glad of it: 'I couldn't bear to be idle just now,' he wrote in May. His friend and partner Tommy Nelson and his brother Alastair had lately been killed in the Battle of Arras, Raymond Asquith had fallen on the Somme the year before, Bron

'The Front Line, Saint Eloi' (1917), by Paul Nash, after he had been commissioned as a war artist.

Herbert had been shot down behind the enemy lines. One side of the job was propaganda to the enemy and to neutral countries; the other, and to Buchan the more important, was the promotion of national unity at home. 'In a contest of whole peoples,' he wrote, 'psychology must be a matter of prime importance.' As he had tried in his articles for *The Times*, so now, through film and painting as well as the press, he tried to bridge the gaps between the fighting men and the non-combatants at home.

It was Charles Masterman – ex-Liberal minister and old friend of Buchan – who first thought of commissioning artists to record the war. Buchan, who had been much struck by Paul Nash's paintings of the Ypres salient, took up the idea with enthusiasm. Nash was sent back to the Front to paint, not to fight, and other artists were commissioned: among them were Sargent, Wilson Steer, Orpen, Muirhead Bone and James McBey, whose etchings record Allenby's campaign in Palestine.

The outstanding film commissioned by the ministry was *The Battle of the Somme*. No civilian in his local picture-house, seeing those thin lines of tired soldiers squelching through the mud, those terrible piles of dead, the company ready to go over the top – and reminded by the titles that ten minutes after the pictures were taken these men were under heavy fire – could plead ignorance of the ordeal his son or his neighbour or his workmate was enduring on the Western Front.

Professional writers were brought in to play their part too: one of Buchan's first actions at the ministry had been to cable Hugh Walpole, then in Petrograd, and offer him a job. Anthony Hope, Henry Newbolt and Arnold Bennett were on the staff too, and other writers were invited to visit the Fronts and report their impressions. Thomas Hardy was one of those who regretted he could not accept; he was too old, he said, and his military expertise was really of the 'flint-lock and touch-hole period' – but he asked if he might keep the passport form which Buchan had sent him, 'to show what I was on the brink of doing at 77'.

Missionaries were also dispatched to America where, even after the United States entered the war, there was much anti-British feeling, and even more ignorance about the fighting the British had done; many newspapers gave the impression that the war was being fought by France and Canada. Heavily censored war news was not enough to engage American sympathies, so Buchan set up a Department of Information in New York, sent out lecturers who could speak of the fighting at first hand, and invited influential Americans to come over and see for themselves.

Propaganda to enemy countries involved, among other things, smuggling, forging, and dropping miniature pamphlets by balloon, activities bordering on those of the intelligence departments. Opinion in and out of the Buchan family varies as to whether Buchan himself was directly involved in secret service work; but it is clear that he had plenty to do with those who were. 'Correspondents and secret service agents till all hours,' he noted in a letter of May 1917 – perhaps these operated something like the underground system that whisked Blenkiron, Hannay and Mary from the Alps to the Western Front in *Mr Standfast*, which Buchan began to write in the summer of 1917. In another of his fictions, *The Three Hostages*, he makes the detective Macgillivray expound the power of propaganda: 'Have you ever considered what a diabolical weapon that can be – using all the channels of modern publicity to poison and warp men's minds? . . . You can use it cleanly – as I think on the whole we did in the War.'

There was plenty of interest in a job that brought Buchan close to Lloyd George and Balfour, Admiral Beatty and Field-Marshal Robertson, Jan Smuts and the powerful Director of Naval Intelligence, Sir Reginald Hall. But there was plenty of irritation too – from the jealousies of established ministries, the battles to extract information from the Service departments (which could be sticky to the point of hostility), from 'the continuous struggle with small-mindedness and pettiness'. On top of such strains and stresses there was the labour of keeping the Nelson *History of the War* up to date; Buchan had a research assistant, but the actual writing was all his own. His home life, too, was disjointed for, in view of the air-raids over London, he had urged Susan to take the children to the country for long stretches. (There were now three – William was born in 1916; Alastair, the fourth and last, in September 1918.) Adding to the general strain, and no doubt aggravated by it, was Buchan's troublesome inside. But he battled on, feeling, as so many civilians did then and in the next war, that any effort that might shorten the actual fighting by as much as a minute was worth any price in exhaustion and discomfort. A week after the Armistice one of his colleagues, taking admiring leave of his chief, summed up the result of their labours: 'Public opinion was undoubtedly influenced, we have proof upon proof of that. And public opinion just meant everything to the Allied cause.'

After four years of war and disrupted family life, John and Susan had daydreams of settling peacefully in a little grey manor-house in the Cotswolds, where the children could roam the countryside and fish; but this Elysium must also be within daily reach of Nelson's office in London. Elsfield Manor, which they acquired in 1919, answered most of their requirements. Elsfield was a small village on a hill, four miles from Oxford and a good railway service to London – though, being in a patch of England which, as Buchan put it, 'the tides of modernity had somehow missed', many of its inhabitants had never been on a train.

The manor was a roomy house of Cotswold stone – a bit top-heavy with a Victorian addition to the original seventeenth-century building – which, like Broughton Green, opened straight on to the village street. On the other side it commanded a splendid view over Eynsham and Witney to the western Cotswolds, forty miles of England on a clear day. It had further charms for its new owner in that the site had been mentioned in Domesday Book, and the house had been visited in 1754 by Dr Johnson. He had walked up from Oxford to take tea with Francis Wise, the Radcliffe Librarian, who during his ownership had done much to improve and ornament the grounds. Here the Buchans happily put down their roots and felt, like Richard Hannay with Fosse Manor, that they were 'anchored at last in the pleasantest kind of harbour'.

It was a house where the successful writer and publisher could delightfully entertain his friends (though he rather overestimated the quality of the rough shooting that went with it). More important, it gave Buchan two things that meant more to him than being a good host. First, it gave him a countryside to belong to. As at Broughton, he

Elsfield Manor, from the garden side. Buchan used to liken it to Horace's villa, 'a small country-house, frugal but with good wine in the cellar and silver, well-rubbed, on the table'.

NON·INFERIORA·SECUTUS·

JOHN·BUCHAN
ELSFIELD·MANOR
OXFORDSHIRE

E·H·NEW   1926

Buchan's bookplate: the old Buchan motto, 'Following nothing base', was adopted for his coat of arms when he became a baron.

'The war left me with an intense craving for country life': a stretch of the Oxfordshire countryside where Buchan put down his roots.

could step out of the house and within a few minutes be deep in the country. Sometimes he walked, sometimes he rode his old hunter Alan Breck, often he took his rod with him. In the woods about Beckley and Noke, remnants of the old forest, on the marshy ground of Otmoor, on the banks of Windrush or Cherwell, he was in real country, unsuburbanized, unprettified, rich in rare birds and wild flowers, that was earning its living in the traditional ways, and whose character and people he grew to appreciate as he had those of Tweeddale. It was still the pastoral and poetic Oxfordshire of his undergraduate days. His daughter Alice remembers how, when she was riding with him, he would rein in on the crest of Elsfield Hill and recite the verse from *Thyrsis* with the lines about the Fyfield elm, then still conspicuous on the Berkshire skyline. She, too, knew the poem by heart, but would listen obligingly to her father's recitation, and try not to think of tea.

Second, Elsfield gave Buchan back many of the pleasures of that golden age, his own Oxford years. Soon after he had bought it he was invited by Lord Curzon, Chancellor of the University, to become a Curator of the University Chest. This not very onerous function gave Buchan a standing in the university; and as he had kept up his membership of the Union and of Vincent's Club, he would often dine in one or the other after meetings, or before addressing an undergraduate society, or taking part in its business. (He was invited to be treasurer of the Conservative Association, and president of the Exploration Club.) He was delighted to meet the new crop of university wits, scholars, politicians and explorers, who would be bidden up to Elsfield where the Buchans kept open house on Sunday afternoons. (The aesthetes and writers were more likely to be off to Lady Ottoline Morrell's at Garsington.) In the gay and lively talk, in the intellectual high spirits, in the hopeful plans for the future, Buchan could recapture something of the Oxford he had known with Raymond Asquith, Aubrey Herbert, Cubby Medd and Tommy Nelson. Just when middle age was setting in, this new generation made him feel young again.

As for the young, who over the years included many who were to make their political mark as MPs, ministers and ambassadors – Robert Boothby, John Strachey, Alan Lennox-Boyd, Quintin Hogg, Evelyn Baring, Frank Pakenham, Roger Makins – they found it well worth the four-mile walk or bicycle ride. The tea itself was a proper meal, with a profusion of home-made scones and cakes, not a matter of a thin sandwich and a biscuit. In summer it was delightful to stroll in the garden, where asparagus beds coexisted with peonies, potatoes with roses, and where Mr Wise's temple still stood. In winter there was the

Robert Boothby, one of the young men who walked up from Oxford to Elsfield for an ample tea and lively talk.

library, with the portrait of Sir Walter Raleigh over the mantelpiece, and Buchan on the hearth-rug, hands behind him, rocking on his heels, courteously listening, then happily launching himself into the argument. 'He would stand and face you and discuss endlessly,' one visitor recalled, 'wedge-nosed, his head forward and to one side, his lips parted, eager to speak, eager to listen. I do not remember that he ever broke off a conversation.'

There would be senior visitors too: old friends like the Gilbert Murrays, now living on Boar's Hill, and W. P. Ker, the Professor of Poetry, who liked walking up to Elsfield as Johnson had done; new friends like T. E. Lawrence, riding up on his powerful motorcycle (itself more of an attraction to the Buchan boys than the hero of the revolt in the desert) and Robert Graves from Islip. Staying in the house would be guests from farther away. Many a useful contact between aspiring politician and established statesman (like L. S. Amery) or between embryo historian and great scholar (like G. M. Trevelyan) was made over the tea-table at Elsfield.

Every spring Mrs Buchan and Anna came for a visit. Anna, as O. Douglas, was now an acclaimed and successful novelist. Buchan was

T.E. Lawrence (1888–1935) and his famous motorcycle, with George Brough, its maker.

Opposite: In the library at Elsfield.

Sir Henry Newbolt (left), a man much loved by Buchan, and Sir James Barrie, a man for whose writings Buchan had no relish, on their way to receive honorary degrees at Oxford in 1926.

proud and pleased about his sister's success, and his children loved her. But with their grandmother they felt some unease. When they went to the village church, she said they were being tainted with Anglicanism, and she taunted their father with bowing in the house of Rimmon – which Alice envisaged as one of the redbrick houses in north Oxford. They tried hard not to provoke her by any excessive Englishness, and they could wholeheartedly appreciate her feather-light scones – 'You could eat a dozen at a sitting and not feel full.'

Among the Buchan children's favourite visitors were the poet Henry Newbolt and his wife. When they came, the evenings would be given up to poetry, Newbolt and Buchan reading aloud in turn – Buchan at some point declaiming Victor Hugo's *Chasseur Noir* with great feeling. Alice, now developing her own literary tastes, thought there was too much Belloc and Chesterton and Calverley; fresh from grappling with Wyndham Lewis, Spengler and Ezra Pound, she was rather severe on her father's penchant for light verse. But when he was reading his own latest novel to the family, it was pure pleasure.

There was a new one every year from 1922 to 1936; many of them, from *The Three Hostages* to *The Island of Sheep*, reflected the pleasures and activities of the Buchans' holidays during those years: climbing and stalking and fishing in Mull and Morvern and Wester Ross; fishing and bird-watching (with Johnnie outstripping his father as an ornithologist) in the Shetlands and Faeroes. Earlier holidays were recalled too. In *The Dancing Floor* Buchan revisited the Aegean Islands where he had cruised in 1910; in *Huntingtower* and *Castle Gay* he was back in Galloway and Carrick, where he had walked and climbed in his university vacations. *Witch Wood* took him back to his boyhood country – but three centuries earlier, when the great forest of Caledon

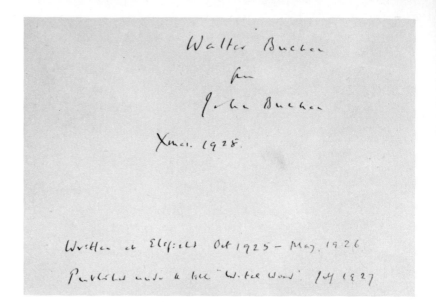

Walter Buchan
from
John Buchan
Xmas. 1928.

Written at Elsfield Oct 1925 – May. 1926
Published under the title "Witch Wood" July 1927

The manuscript of *Witch Wood*, inscribed for Walter Buchan. This novel about Tweeddale in the seventeenth century was originally called 'The Minister of Woodilee'.

covered the upper Tweed. In the other historical tales, *Midwinter* and *The Blanket of the Dark*, he was exploring the past of his own Oxfordshire countryside.

There was also a steady flow of other books. As soon as the war was over, Buchan had drawn up a timetable for work to be done in the next two years.* It was as detailed as those he had drawn up in Glasgow and at Oxford, and was as successfully carried through. There were three headings, 'Main Work', 'Second String', 'Third String'; for January to March 1920 it went like this:

Main Work – Finish Path of a K[ing].
Second String – Finish South African War Record [he had been commissioned to write the history of the South African Forces in France].
Third String – Begin Greeks and Northmen [a projected series of lectures].

It was a high rate of work for a man who was not a full-time writer, and he kept it up through the 'twenties and 'thirties with four major biographies – of Montrose, Scott, Cromwell and Augustus – to show that Buchan the scholar could do as well in his line as Buchan the storyteller in *his*. Yet he never seems to have thought of dedicating his whole time and energy to writing. He had it in him to be a writer of the

---

*Another scribbled agenda in the same notebook mixes practical duties with literary. Before the end of June 1919, for instance, he planned to 'Publish *Mr Standfast*; Publish *These for Remembrance*; LL.D; KCB; Settle Elsfield; Arrange for house in Oxford [while the builders were in Elsfield]; Revise *History of the War* to the end of Chapter III; Write South African record to the end of the Battle of Arras; Begin Grenfell book; Arrange for moving of furniture.' He was later able to tick off each item, including the LL.D (from St Andrew's in 1930), except the KCB – an honour he would have liked in recognition of his work at the Ministry of Information, and which he had been encouraged to expect.

first class, but his other ambitions kept him from concentrating on this single aim (and, as if in self-excuse, he could be quite sniffy about professional writers and literary gatherings).

Surveying his own work near the end of his life, Buchan took little credit for the thrillers, which 'I never consciously invented with a pen in my hand; I waited until the story had told itself and then wrote it down, and since it was already a finished thing, I wrote it fast'. More conscious creation had gone into the historical romances, which he rated more highly. 'Being equally sensitive to the spells of time and of space, to a tract of years and a tract of landscape, I tried to discover the historical moment which best interpreted the *ethos* of a particular countryside, and to devise the appropriate legend.' His biographies had been 'laborious affairs compared to my facile novels', but had given him the greatest satisfaction of all. Two certainly are likely to endure, those where he enters imaginatively into the lives of the two Scots whom he had loved since boyhood – Scott and Montrose.

Yet it is the thrillers which have appealed most to modern readers, appearing and reappearing in paperback, often with luridly inappropriate pictures on the cover. It is from them that phrases like 'a Buchan hero' and 'a Buchan adventure' derive. What gives them their

The Marquis of Montrose, after the picture painted by Honthorst for the Queen of Bohemia. Soldier, poet, a Presbyterian Cavalier, Montrose had been Buchan's hero since childhood; he wrote a biography of him in 1913, and thoroughly revised and enlarged it in 1928. *Montrose* is his outstanding achievement as a biographer and, as he told a friend, 'contains most of my philosophy of life'.

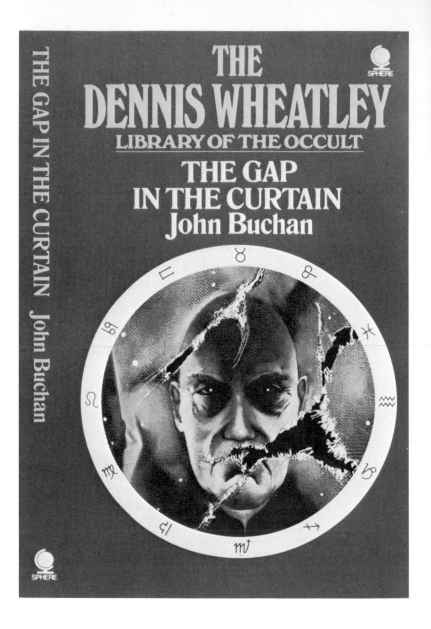

Buchan's *Gap in the Curtain,*
published soberly by Hodder and
Stoughton in 1932, made a startling
reappearance in 1974.

continuing vitality is something over and above Buchan's mastery of
the standard thriller ingredients – suspense, surprise, speed of narrative,
well-observed background. It is his ability to touch deeper concerns
than the triumph of hero or the fall of villain. He can convey a sense of
the real possibility of evil and irrational forces breaking through the
façade of civilized life. Many of the social attitudes of his thrillers are
outdated; not so their intimations of destruction and disorder, their
warning that civilization cannot be taken for granted. In 1940 Graham
Greene found that 'Buchan prepared us in his thrillers better than he

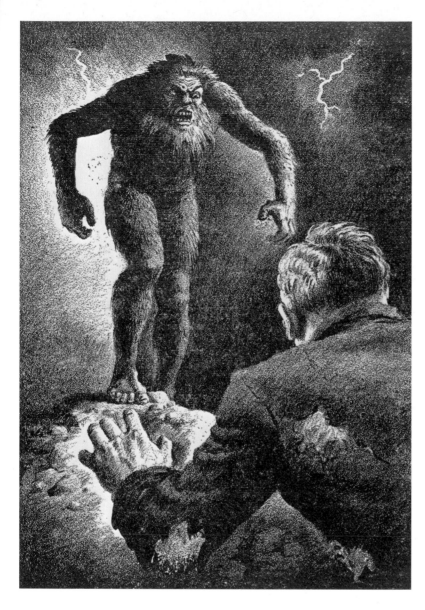

Buchan's story 'No-Man's Land', written when he was at Oxford, and collected in *The Watcher by the Threshold* (1902), was reprinted in *Famous Fantastic Mysteries* of December 1949. The illustrator allowed his imagination free rein on the figure of the Pict who survived underground to frighten the life out of Mr Graves, the Fellow of St Chad's, Oxford, whose interest in primitive peoples took him to the lonely moors of Galloway, where to his horror he found them.

knew for the death that may come to any of us, as it nearly came to Leithen, by the railings of the Park or the doorway of the mews. For certainly we can all see now "how thin is the protection of civilization".' The kidnapping of children of the rich and powerful is not as unthinkable in the later part of the twentieth century as it was to the original readers of *The Three Hostages*.

Buchan still hankered after a political career though, in the years immediately after the war, he made no effort to become a parliamentary candidate. Only a Scottish seat appealed to him; and now that he was settled in Oxfordshire, he had no wish to be involved in the extra burden of nursing a constituency beyond the border. In 1927, however, came the opportunity of a Scottish seat without this burden, on the death of Sir Henry Craik, one of the three MPs representing the Scottish universities. Practically all that was demanded of a candidate was to compose an election address (voting for the now abolished university seats was by post); practically all that was demanded of an elected member was to show an interest in education, and in Scottish affairs. Buchan was delighted, especially because a university member could sit fairly loose to party. He beat his Labour opponent in the by-election by 16,903 to 2,378, and in the election of 1929 he topped the poll in all four Scottish universities.

Although Buchan's maiden speech (in July 1927, on a Conservative proposal to increase the powers of the House of Lords, which he opposed) was loudly acclaimed, and though his later speeches always drew a good attendance, he was not generally considered to be a very effective Parliamentarian. He talked knowledgeably and well on a variety of subjects, from Scottish home rule (he was sympathetic to its supporters, but opposed to a separate Parliament) to supposed left-wing infiltration of the BBC (in his view a mare's nest, invented by diehard Tories); but he had no parliamentary achievement to his credit to match that of another university member, A. P. Herbert, in getting his divorce Bill on to the statute book.

One of Buchan's parliamentary activities seems especially worth mentioning. He was chairman of the Pro-Palestine Committee in the House of Commons, and a friend and ally of the Zionists in the House. He wrote and spoke with enthusiasm and sympathy of Jewish immigrants to Palestine, and was critical of what he considered the British administration's obstructive attitude. 'When I think of Zionism,' he wrote, 'I think of it in the first place as a great act of justice. It is reparation for the centuries of cruelty and wrong which have stained the record of nearly every Gentile people.' His name was written in the Golden Book of the Jewish National Fund of Israel, to be honoured along with such other friends of Israel as Smuts, Balfour, Amery and Orde Wingate.

This activity of Buchan's is seldom remembered by critics eager to picture him as an antisemite. They base their case on derogatory references to Jews in the novels, particularly *The Three Hostages*. I dealt at some length with this matter in my biography of Buchan, and Gertrude Himmelfarb and David Daniell have also discussed it. The two points I would make here are that many of the slighting references are made by characters in the novels who would (however regrettably) be likely to talk in such a way, and are not to be taken as Buchan himself talking; and that there are sympathetic portraits of Jews in his fiction (for instance Lowenstein in *A Lodge in the Wilderness,* Lawson in the early tale *The Grove of Ashtaroth*). Buchan disliked many of the Jews he had seen flaunting their wealth in Johannesburg or Park Lane, and he could generalize carelessly, as we have all painfully learnt not to. But his carelessness is outmatched by the carelessness of the critics who take account of only a small part of the evidence about his attitude.

For European affairs, Buchan had a distaste shared by many who had endured and survived the 1914–18 war, which had killed their friends and brothers. Never again, he passionately believed, could there be a repetition of its horror, folly and waste. Revulsion from such a possibility inclined him to see Hitler and Mussolini more as ridiculous aberrations – 'a couple of lunatics', 'this tom-fool Nazi rule' – than as ever-growing menaces to the peace of Europe. He was quick to protest at the early signs of Hitler's persecution of the Jews – in May 1934 he spoke at a mass protest meeting in Shoreditch – but he could not bring himself to believe that even Hitler could contemplate the risk of all-out war in Europe.

During the parliamentary session, Buchan spent three or four nights a week in London. Susan and Alice would join him for a month or two in the summer, renting a house in Westminster; the rest of the time Buchan stayed with his mother-in-law or in the St Stephen's Club. He was often bidden to parties at Londonderry House – both the huge political crushes, and the more intimate gatherings called by Lady Londonderry her Ark. Churchill, Ramsay MacDonald and the Irish writers Sean O'Casey and James Stephens were often present, known by the names of animals bestowed by their hostess, who called herself Circe. But most of Buchan's evenings were spent in the House, where he was generally popular, with as many friends on the other side as on his own.

The two groups he most enjoyed were the younger Tories and the Clydesiders. With Harold Macmillan, Robert Boothby, W. S. Morrison, Walter Elliot – independent-minded Tories for whom Conservatism was a matter of ideas and principles rather than class interest and party tactics, Buchan was very much at home. So, too, in a different way, with the Clydesiders. They might send shivers up the spine of the Tory diehards, but to Buchan they were men from a familiar world. Jimmy Maxton – with his pale face and long hair the very pattern of a revolutionary, but too gentle and too indolent (so thought Emanuel Shinwell) ever to lead a mob – had been like Buchan at Hutchesons' Grammar School and at Glasgow University, where Tom Johnston too had graduated. George Buchanan, member for the Gorbals, had been born in the district, not far from the Rev. John Buchan's kirk. Buchan would join them and John McGovern and David Kirkwood, in the library for a late-night cup of tea (most of

Lady Londonderry, the 'Circe' of her circle of intimates, who often entertained Buchan, in his parliamentary days, at Londonderry House in Park Lane. Here she is seen unveiling a statue of Dom Perignon at Rheims on the 250th anniversary of his discovery of how to put the sparkle into champagne.

these wild Clydesiders were teetotal) and for talk of Glasgow, fishing, Scottish history, the part that Scots had played in the Empire; and his voice would lose some of the 'manse intonation' his critics had noted, and take on some of the accent that often made the Clydesiders hard for the English to understand. In their view, Buchan was a decent man who had got into the wrong party.

The historian A. L. Rowse, who in his early left-wing days was a regular visitor to Elsfield, was much struck by the 'extraordinary catholicism' of Buchan's political sympathies. 'In fact, I believe it was a special recommendation with him that one was on the other side.' This interest in political ideas, of whatever colour, could be an asset when Buchan was drawn in to help with the educational activities of

James Maxton (1885–1946), 'who not only preached the revolution but looked it', and George Buchanan (1890–1955), two of the MPs for Clydeside constituencies who had started like Buchan from Glasgow's south side but whose path to Westminster had been very different from his.

the Conservative Party – he was involved in the setting-up of the Bonar Law College at Ashridge, for short-term courses for Conservative agents and candidates, where the keynote was political education, not party propaganda. Nor did his independence do him any harm in his academic constituency, whose graduate voters could appreciate his voting on the merits of any particular measure rather than on rigid party lines. But his lack of party zeal did not recommend him to the party managers; and his limited interest in political manoeuvre, and limited aptitude for it, reduced his effectiveness in the day-to-day realities of Parliament.

The political role which perhaps suited Buchan best was that of confidant and go-between, especially with Stanley Baldwin and

Stanley Baldwin (1867–1947), Prime Minister when Buchan entered the House of Commons in 1927, and Ramsay MacDonald (1866–1937), Prime Minister from 1929, first of a Labour Government, then, after the economic crisis of 1931, of a National Government. Buchan, who knew them both well, admired Baldwin for his tolerant conservatism and shared many of his literary tastes; in MacDonald he saw a man of courage and principle who in 1931 had put the national need above party loyalty, and had been repaid by his party's ostracism. 'The whole man was a romance, almost an anachronism. To understand him one had to understand the Scottish Celt, with his ferocious pride, his love of pageantry and poetry, his sentiment about the past, his odd contradictory loyalties.'

Ramsay MacDonald. For Baldwin – that moderate, conciliatory Tory, Prime Minister till 1929, Leader of the Opposition to 1931 then second-in-command to Ramsay MacDonald in the National Government – Buchan had much liking and admiration. Baldwin reciprocated – though he may have valued Buchan more as friend and writer than as active politician. He liked talking things over with Buchan, he found him useful as negotiator and drafter of speeches, and after 1931 he enlisted Buchan's help on the ever-present need of keeping up the Prime Minister's morale. For Ramsay MacDonald, disowned and regarded as a traitor by all but a handful of the Labour Party for having joined the Tories in a National Government, was in a lonely and exposed position. Buchan was drawn to him as a Scot who had risen from a Lossiemouth cottage to 10 Downing Street by hard work and force of personality; and he admired him for, as he saw it, putting country before party in the crisis of 1931. So he was very ready to help – by pre-breakfast walks in St James's Park, when he lent a sympathetic ear to the Prime Minister's problems and worries, and by drafting speeches – though MacDonald could ruin any draft by interpolating a few metaphors, and then wildly mixing them. (At the Prime Minister's request, Buchan drafted the address delivered by the Speaker in Westminster Hall on King George V's jubilee in 1935.) Buchan was disappointed at not being offered a post in the National

Government of 1931, or in the later reshuffles; but he was near the centre of things, he was in the know.

This busy man, this writer-cum-politician-cum-country gentleman, was a puzzle to many. How did he fit it all in? 'He is a thoroughly organised man,' Arnold Bennett noted in his Journal for 7 March 1928: 'John Buchan, invited for tea at 4.30, arrived at 4.27. He had a Committee Meeting for 5.30. And at 5.15 he simply got up and left.' To his countrymen, he presented more complex questions. One young Scot, hearing him lecture at Oxford, was dismayed by the precise figure 'with the hybrid accent of the Anglified Scot'.

Is this the wonderful pagan of *The Grove of Ashtaroth*, the man who revels in travel and enterprise? And where, between the adventurer and the man of affairs, does the elder of St Columba's fit in? Who is this person who wears so many masks, and under which mask may he himself be found?

Another Scot has described how she had to overcome suspicions aroused by the public image of this successful fellow-countryman. She was Catherine Carswell, friend and biographer of D. H. Lawrence, and author of a life of Burns which Buchan much admired. One day in 1932 he invited her to lunch.

I was to be in the lounge of a small restaurant in Jermyn Street promptly at one o'clock. My host would be coming from the House of Commons with little time to spare.

I arrived a couple of minutes before time. But he was before me – in both senses. There he sat under the clock in the lounge on a sort of sofa covered with red velvet. Rather, he was disposed there in a posture of the most admirable relaxation, his head leaning against the high back of the seat, his eyes closed.

I had sometimes wondered how he managed to get through his many and varied undertakings . . . How did he compass it all? He had, as I then but vaguely knew, suffered from illness. He looked a frail being here before me, unconscious as yet of my presence. I found, however, at least part answer to my question. He is always the first, I reflected, at any rendezvous. He uses the extra minutes to rest every nerve and muscle. At this moment his mind is emptied of everything except the brief opportunity for repose or meditation.

The picture I had carried away from his public appearance was of a man spare, even meagre; precise, even prim; compressed in manner and movement. His speech, somewhat clipped and – to a critical Scottish ear – synthetic, had confirmed this impression. A cautious correctness had seemed in him to be personified. Here, at close quarters and in a light at once more intimate and more exposed, he gained immeasurably. His face was revealed as 'fine-drawn' – to use one of his own favourite terms of description – in lines of energy and fatigue, sensibility and asceticism, recklessness and reserve; fastidious lines composing a delicate harmony of contradictions which lost very much with distance. The scar from an accident in childhood drew attention to the strikingly noble contours of his head. The long, queer nose, questing and sagacious as a terrier's, was in odd contrast with the lean,

The member for the Scottish universities, in his London uniform.

The family on holiday in the Brecon Beacons in 1930. Standing: Buchan and his mother. Sitting: Alastair, William, Susan Buchan, Johnnie, Anna Buchan (O. Douglas) and Alice.

The Conspirator: with Alice, as they were to appear in a play of hers about Guy Fawkes, in Oxford in 1930.

scholarly cheeks and with the mouth narrowed as by concentration or the hint of pain subdued. A peculiar countenance, subtle, in no respect trivial . . .

From time to time I had heard it suggested that this man was something of a careerist; worthy, of course, and admirable, but with something of what the term might imply of distaste. Those who made the suggestion – usually fellow-Scots of less luxurious attainment than his – had not the smallest personal acquaintance with him. It was perhaps natural that they should see in him the typical, never wholly sympathetic hero of the 'success story'. Such a verdict has little weight, but it was not for me wholly contradicted by his public appearances. Add to this that his tastes in men and books had seemed to be as contrary to mine as were his politics . . . In that moment, however, I was divested of all prejudice. Here he was, a man of my own generation and country, all unknowing under my regard. I had been interested; I became disposed to friendliness without reservations. At the same time I was also conscious to an acute degree that we should presently be talking together – of what?

The clock struck one. His eyes opened and saw me. He sprang up smiling, without a hint of lassitude, to make me welcome.

What they were presently talking about was Buchan's wish to be a kind of godfather to Catherine Carswell's son, and help with his education. 'He did everything to make it seem that I, not he, was the donor. He made it not merely impossible to refuse but easy and natural to accept.'

Catherine Carswell's experience was that of many others – they found Buchan so much more likable in reality than the widespread image of a careerist had led them to expect. His foibles were obvious: his liking for titles, his easily-claimed familiarity with the great and famous. But the many to whom he gave unobtrusively and unstintedly of his time, concern and money, knew that these foibles were superficial matters, and did not touch the core of his character.

In 1933 Buchan was offered a position which, though of no political importance, greatly appealed to him: High Commissioner to the General Assembly of the Church of Scotland. The High Commissioner represents the Sovereign and, for the duration of the assembly, is given royal standing. For ten days he lives in Holyrood, has a military guard of honour and a staff of Pursebearer and ADCs, is addressed as Your Grace. He drives with his escort to the Assembly Hall on the Mound, and speaks at the opening and closing sessions. He visits schools and hospitals, opens charity fêtes, makes innumerable speeches and – at vast dinner-parties at Holyrood, and a garden-party – entertains members of the Assembly and people of consequence from all over Scotland. After some initial doubts over expense, Buchan was delighted to accept. He enjoyed reigning in Holyrood, if only for ten days, after which, Cinderella-like, His Grace reverted to John Buchan.

Their Graces the High Commissioner and Mrs Buchan with their family, their guests and their suite at Holyrood in 1934.

His gentle father had never made any great stir beyond his own parish; now Buchan, the first minister's son to be High Commissioner, was being received in style by the Kirk assembled. It was a moving experience for him and for his mother and sister Anna, who stayed at Holyrood for the whole ten days.

Old friends in Scotland could be tart or amused by Buchan's quasi-royal style; but the general opinion was that he had acquitted himself well, and he was invited to be High Commissioner again in 1934. The experience could be considered a sort of dry-run for his next appointment: Governor-General of Canada.

When Buchan was invited to go – and the invitation came from Canada, for since 1930 it had been on the Dominion Prime Minister's advice that such Crown appointments were made – he drew up a list of pros and cons. The reasons against included 'Too easy a job for a comparatively young man' (he was not yet sixty) and 'A week further away from Mother'. Those for included 'A very easy life for J.B.', 'The possibility of doing good work', and the fact that 'Apart from special clothes and uniforms we could do it on our salary and the rest of our income would mount up.' Susan's reckoning was different. She hated the whole idea of a life lived largely in public, of playing a role determined by others, of leaving Elsfield and her work with the Women's Institutes, of being a week's journey farther from the children. (Johnnie was now in the Colonial Service in Uganda; Alice, married to Brian Fairfax-Lucy, was living near Burford; Billy was working in films in London, and Alastair was still at Eton.) She was increasingly worried about her husband's health, and not a bit sure that it would be 'A very easy life for J.B.' – though they would be much more together than had been possible in his parliamentary years. But when he came down on the Yes side, she would not stand in his way. Old Mrs Buchan was delighted – though her first comment, 'I am sure the King is fortunate to get you', implied that her brilliant son was conferring, as well as receiving, honour. Her pleasure was enhanced when he was made a baron, and took his title of Tweedsmuir from the country where she had been born and where he had always been happy and entirely at home.

On 2 November 1935, the new Governor-General landed at Wolfe's Cove in a blood-red sunset, to be received by the Chief Justice of Canada and by the Prime Minister, Mackenzie King. In gathering darkness they drove up the Rock in a horse-drawn carriage, escorted by cavalry through the cobbled streets of Quebec to Parliament House, where Tweedsmuir was sworn in. He was wearing a uniform which Vincent Massey – who inherited it when he became Governor-General – described as 'rather Duke of Wellington style – two rows of buttons – tails – epaulets of silver lace – plumed cocked hat like a

W.L. Mackenzie King
(1874–1950), Prime Minister of
Canada during Tweedsmuir's
Governor-Generalship.

general's'. Tweedsmuir carried the Royal Commission, dated 10
August – the delay in arrival was due to the Canadian general election
that October. He also carried with him, under that plumed hat, an
interest in Canada of long standing.

During his years on the *Spectator* he had written much and
appreciatively about the country ('Canada is essentially a country of the
larger air, where men can still face the old primeval forces of Nature
and be braced into vigour, and withal so beautiful that it can readily
inspire that romantic patriotism which is one of the most priceless assets
of a people'). In his Nelson *History of the War*, Buchan had followed
the actions of the Canadian forces, helped in this by talks with General
Byng (whom he had first known in South Africa and who became
Governor-General of Canada in 1921). Soon after the war he had
written the life of Lord Minto, Governor-General from 1898 to 1904.
In 1924 he visited Canada, staying first at Laurier House in Ottawa
with Mackenzie King (then, as later, Prime Minister), afterwards with

On the Ramparts of the Citadel, Quebec, during the visit of the President of the United States in July 1936: Tweedsmuir, Mackenzie King, Franklin D. Roosevelt and his son James.

Governor-General Byng at Rideau Hall. He was much in demand to speak and lecture, and he was much liked; his audiences could find nothing in him of that attitude of unconscious superiority often displayed by visiting Englishmen. Over the years Buchan had learned much of the forces, natural and human, that had shaped Canada. He had a sense of its past and of the present currents of political activity and aspiration, an enthusiasm for its rivers, mountains and wilds and an eagerness to see them for himself; and a conviction of the country's enormous possibilities.

'A high office,' T. E. Lawrence had written on his appointment, 'to which I grudge you immensely. You are too good to become a figure.' A figure he had to be, and at times a very ceremonial one. There were state occasions, like the opening of Parliament; the formal receptions at Rideau Hall; the state visits, as of Franklin Roosevelt to Quebec in 1936 – the first time an American President had officially visited Canada – and the return visit to Washington next year, with Tweedsmuir receiving all the honours due to a head of state. He enjoyed the ceremony of such occasions (as Susan did not) and was not

irked by matters of protocol or precedence. He performed well, as he had at Holyrood; he meant to cut a good figure, but he intended to be much more than a figure. He was determined that the formal duties of a Governor-General were only the beginning of his real work in Canada, that the things he had to do should be made the opportunities for the things he most wished to do.

Of his Victorian predecessor Lord Durham, he had once written: 'He had that first quality of a great Proconsul, that he passionately identified himself with the land he governed.' There was no question now of 'governing', as there had been in Durham's day; but Tweedsmuir could identify himself with the country to which he was called. And the first step was to learn everything he could about Canada and Canadians.

The Governor-General's chief residence, Rideau Hall, is a couple of miles from the centre of Ottawa, by the Rideau River: a handsome stone mansion set in a wooded park full of chipmunks and squirrels, and big enough for Tweedsmuir's brisk daily walks. There were also

Rideau Hall, Ottawa, the official residence of the Governor-General.

official quarters in the Citadel at Quebec, beyond the barrack square, where the Tweedsmuirs spent a few weeks every year. It was nowhere as spacious as Rideau Hall, the rooms were small and snug, but there were marvellous views over the St Lawrence. Susan was happiest there.

The household at Rideau Hall was large. The Tweedsmuirs had brought out from Britain James Cast and Amos Webb, their Elsfield butler and chauffeur, and a number of footmen and housemaids (some recruited from royal households). Mrs Killick, his personal secretary since the early days at Nelson's, had come too. His official staff included the Secretary, Shuldham Redfern, fresh from governing a province in the Sudan; the Comptroller, Lt-Col. Eric Mackenzie; a lady-in-waiting; and four ADCs. The senior was a Canadian, Willis O'Connor, who had been appointed by Byng and who stayed with the Tweedsmuirs throughout: a humorous, outgoing man, who seemed to know everyone in Canada – knowledge that was invaluable to a new Governor-General. Willis O'Connor organized the ADCs' work: the other three took it in turns to attend His Excellency, or Her Excellency, or take a week off. These junior ADCs served for a year or two: among those who held the post in Tweedsmuir's time were Michael Adeane (later Private Secretary to Queen Elizabeth II), David Walker, the author of *Geordie* and other novels, and Tom Goff the maker of harpsichords. Tweedsmuir always preferred young men

A room in the Governor-General's other residence, at the Citadel, Quebec, which stands on a bluff overlooking the St Lawrence. Susan Tweedsmuir felt most at home here: 'when I lay awake at night I could hear, like strophe and antistrophe, the hooting of tugs on the river on one side, and on the other a little bell ringing from one of the convents, summoning the nuns to prayer in the darkest hour of the night.'

with sharp minds and wide interests to the correct, social type of officer often found as an ADC.

Tweedsmuir left his staff to get on with their work, and did not fuss over details. He got through his official papers quickly and, when in Ottawa or Quebec, found more time for his own reading and writing than he had for years. Soon after his arrival he began a biography of the Emperor Augustus: he would write a paragraph or two, then, when an ADC told him it was time to open a hospital or address a society, he would cheerfully get up and go; and, the hospital opened, the speech made, he would return, sit down and go on writing as if there had been no interruption.

In Ottawa, the main ceremony of the year was the opening of Parliament, conducted with the same traditional ritual as at Westminster (with the faithful Commons delaying their entrance to the Senate and chattering as they came in), but with the speech from the Throne being delivered in French as well as English. This was followed by a state banquet and 'drawing-room' at Rideau Hall. There were other banquets and receptions throughout the year, with everyone in full fig and strict protocol observed; but there was plenty of

The Parliament Buildings, Ottawa. Tweedsmuir had an office there where he could talk off the record to senators and MPs.

scope, too, for informal entertaining, lunch-parties and dinners when decorations were not worn, and when the doors of Rideau Hall were open to a wider variety of guests than had been the custom. Travellers, journalists, painters, writers, labour leaders, young people starting out on their careers, anyone with ideas and the ability to talk about them, were all made welcome. Eyebrows were raised when Henry Wise Wood, the militant agrarian leader from Calgary, was invited for the weekend, and when the left-wing young men of the Canadian Co-operative Federation were seen deep in talk with the Governor-General. By bringing all sorts of people under his roof Tweedsmuir made Rideau Hall, in the words of one Canadian, 'a high-class inn at a busy cross-roads'.

To this high-class inn also came a stream of visitors from overseas. They included Dr Bruning, the former Chancellor of Germany – a man of moderation whom Tweedsmuir admired immensely – and Adam von Trott, a young German diplomat who was to be executed in 1944 for his part in the resistance to Hitler; politicians from Britain and America – Cordell Hull, Stanley Baldwin, Duff Cooper; stage people, come to Canada to perform, or to adjudicate in drama festivals – Gertrude Lawrence, Michel St Denis, Harley Granville-Barker, Ruth Draper; and many of the Tweedsmuirs' family and friends. Mrs Buchan and Anna came over in 1936; the old lady, then in her eightieth year, and slightly mellowed, was game for anything: parties, meetings with the Cardinal, visits to Women's Institutes. When Susan, flagging after a hard day's programme, cried off a last-minute request to visit a hospital, her mother-in-law went happily in her place.

Constitutionally, the Governor-General was the link between the Dominion and the King (who, as Tweedsmuir liked to insist, was King of Canada as well as of the United Kingdom) and, like the King, he was entitled to be kept fully informed about his country's politics. Tweedsmuir did not rely only on the information that came through official channels: he went out to learn for himself. This he did by regular visits to his office in Parliament Buildings, where any senator or MP could drop in for talks off the record, by informal sessions with Cabinet ministers and provincial premiers and political journalists over a glass of sherry at Rideau Hall; and mainly by keeping in close touch with the Prime Minister. Tweedsmuir admired Mackenzie King as a politician, though he could never find this strange man, in whom a soft-centred spiritualist and hard-headed party manager uneasily coexisted, really congenial. There were one or two occasions when King thought that the Governor-General had put a foot on forbidden ground – as in a speech at Calgary in 1936 about Canada's defence policy – but Tweedsmuir would quickly apologize, and there were no open rows (as there had been between Mackenzie King and Byng) and usually they rubbed along together well enough.

Tweedsmuir and his mother at Ottawa in the summer of 1936 when she came on a visit with Anna. She died at Bank House the next year.

They were at one in the autumn of 1936 over the problem of Edward VIII and Mrs Simpson. The British Prime Minister needed to know what the Dominion thought of the matter: as the affair had been splashed in American papers which were widely read in Canada, while the British press kept loyally quiet, people in the Dominion were likely to know more about the situation than all but a small circle in Britain, and their views were of special importance. Mackenzie King and Tweedsmuir (who had also been asked to write a letter which could be shown to the King – 'a nice job for a quiet man!') were of one mind in reporting to Baldwin that the feeling in Canada against a possible marriage of the King and a twice-divorced lady was 'deep and serious'. This was partly due to a general disapproval of divorce (particularly among French Canadians), partly to a certain wounded pride that the King – hitherto a popular figure in Canada, and owner of a ranch near Calgary – should be the occasion for all this tattle and scandal in the American press.

Prime Minister and Governor-General were at one, too, as to the importance of good and close relations with the United States, and of Canada's readiness to act as a bridge between America and Europe. It was a triumph for both men when Roosevelt came to Quebec in 1936, though Mackenzie King had some twinges of jealousy at the special relationship that was soon established between Governor-General and President. Tweedsmuir and Roosevelt took to each other at once and talked, off the record, for hours after the formal day's work at Quebec, and on Tweedsmuir's return visit to Washington the next year. Both Tweedsmuir and Mackenzie King were involved in the unofficial talks and exchanges of view which led to Roosevelt's proposal, early in 1938, for a world conference to deal with the problems of Europe that were all too likely to cause another war. When Roosevelt finally put this proposal to Neville Chamberlain, he received an answer 'like a douche of cold water'. This led, among other consequences, to the resignation of his Foreign Secretary, for Anthony Eden (not consulted about the Roosevelt message) had been working for just such an American initiative. (Churchill's comment on the proposal, ten years later, was that 'no event could have been more likely to stave off, or even prevent, war than the arrival of the United States in the circle of European hates and fears'.)

Tweedsmuir was on leave at home during the Czech crisis of 1938. He could not believe that the Munich agreement was any surety of 'peace in our time', as Neville Chamberlain had claimed; it was merely 'a miserable acceptance of the lesser of two evils'. Yet he was profoundly relieved that the precarious peace still held. Anything, almost, would be better than war.

A joint operation which gave Tweedsmuir and Mackenzie King enormous satisfaction was the royal visit of 1939. It was the first time a

reigning monarch had visited a Dominion. It was to be a practical demonstration of the principles of the Statute of Westminster: the King should be seen to be King of Canada, and Canada should be seen to be an independent sovereign power within the association of the Commonwealth. In October 1937 Tweedsmuir, speaking to the Canadian Institute of International Affairs, had affirmed his belief that

Canada is a sovereign nation, and cannot take her attitude to the world docilely from Britain or from the United States or from anybody else. A Canadian's first loyalty is not to the British Commonwealth of Nations, but to Canada, and to Canada's King.

On this occasion of the royal visit there was no jealousy on Mackenzie King's part, for Tweedsmuir considered it constitutionally necessary (as well as personally tactful) to step down at once from his position as the monarch's representative. 'We're out of business,' he told Shuldham Redfern with some relish (though at the King's request he retained certain formal powers of 'The Governor-General in Council',

It was as King and Queen of Canada that George VI and Queen Elizabeth set out on their tour across the country in 1939, while Tweedsmuir ('I cease to exist as Viceroy') kept out of the way. Here they are at Fredericton in New Brunswick, with Prime Minister Mackenzie King (back to the camera) in close attendance.

'I like old and well-tried rods and reels — everything old except the gut'.

which simply meant that he could still sign documents, and not send them chasing after the King on his trip to the Pacific). So when the royal party arrived at Rideau Hall, it was the King and Queen who were the hosts, the Governor-General and his wife the guests. There had been much refurbishing (some redecoration that the Tweedsmuirs had forborne to request for themselves, not wishing to incur an extra charge on the Canadian Government, was now enthusiastically put in hand) and there had to be much reshuffling — the King into the Governor-General's study, the Governor-General into the Secretary's, and the Secretary into a cubby-hole under the stairs. At royal request, the building was now fully equipped with wireless sets.

'It is very important that I myself keep in the background and let Ministers and Lieutenant-Governors run the show, for it is Canada's affair,' Tweedsmuir told his sister; so when the royal party set off on their tour across the Dominion with the Prime Minister in constant attendance, Tweedsmuir took himself off to fish in the Cascapedia River in Quebec. The tour was a great success. In Canada, it gave a

Through the Rockies to British Columbia – a picture taken from the Governor-General's coach, which was attached to one of the regular trains of the Canadian Pacific Railway.

fillip to the sense of nationalism; abroad, it showed Canada in a more independent light. 'The visit,' Tweedsmuir heard from an old friend in London, 'has given Canada a status never quite conceded hitherto. Canada now stands out more distinct from the USA, with her own personality clearly defined.'

Interesting as he found the life in Ottawa, Tweedsmuir was always delighted to be off on tour; and it was on his tours that he really got to know Canada. During his term of office he fairly quartered the country as in his boyhood he had quartered the Border hills. Mostly he went by train (the two official coaches were attached to trains on the regular service) and by boat, though there were some short hops by air. In his first year there were tours through northern and eastern Ontario; to the eastern townships of Quebec; to the northern Prairies and on to British Columbia, then east again by the southern Prairies, suffering their seventh year of drought, and he was back in the Prairies that autumn of 1936. In 1937 there were two tours of the Maritimes, a further visit to the Prairies and to British Columbia, as well as his great journey down the Mackenzie River to the Arctic. In 1938 he was back in the Prairies, to see how the areas most affected by drought were recovering after the spring rains – and found the pastures as green as in Oxfordshire, the wheat springing, and the sloughs full of water. In 1939 with Susan and his brother and sister from Peebles, he went to Churchill on Hudson Bay to meet his son Johnnie, who was working with the Hudson's Bay Company, and had spent a year at their trading post at Cape Dorset. After Churchill came Jasper and the Rockies, and visits to the settlements on the Peace River and the Smoky River of Alberta.

The tours were worked out well in advance with the help of Honorary ADCs (usually retired officers) all over the country. Shuldham Redfern would ask them for suggestions as to what the Governor-General should do and whom he should see, tell them what the Governor-General wanted in the way of rest and diversion, and leave them to work out details of the programmes with mayors, presidents, bishops and other dignitaries of the area they were visiting. There had to be plenty of notice, to allow for a bit of painting and general sprucing-up at the places visited. (One prairie town, taken by surprise, only managed to paint the front of the houses in its main street, and the official route was carefully worked out to avoid any glimpse of a shabby back.)

There was, necessarily, a certain sameness about the incidents of a tour: the reception committee on the station platform, the call at the town hall, the parade of ex-servicemen, the visits to hospital, or barracks or art-gallery; the lunch with the Canada Club (and perhaps tea with the Women's Canada Club – the two bodies could never be persuaded to combine for one party), the dash to the radio station 'to say a few words'. Tweedsmuir was always hoping for a fire-brigade display to liven things up, but was seldom gratified.

Here, to give the flavour of such tours, is the timetable for 12 July 1936, when his party had reached Drumheller in Alberta.

11 a.m. to 12.30 p.m.
 Reception at station. Introduction of Reception Committee, followed by introduction of Messrs. A. M. Charters (one of the oldest, if not the oldest, living ex-soldier in Canada. Mr Charters took part in the 1867 Confederation Ceremonies as a soldier) and E. W. Kendall (centenarian).
 The party will then proceed along station platform to station steps where Guard of Honour of ex-servicemen will be drawn up, together with Girl Guides and Boy Scouts; Inspection of Guard by His Excellency, after which he will unveil the Canadian Legion Cenotaph, and place a wreath on the memorial. Return to train for luncheon.

3 p.m. to 5 p.m.
 Drive round City visiting:

1 Public Library; presentation of pieces of Dinosaur Bone and Petrified Wood.
2 Canadian Utilities Ltd, Plant and Rockery.
3 Rotary Club Swimming Pool.
4 Various Prospect Points.
5 Petrified Wood Locations.
6 At 4.45 p.m. Presentation to His Excellency, on platform near Cenotaph, of a Juniper Root Wood Carving.

Drumheller in Alberta, where the Governor-General carried out a full programme in July 1936.
Tweedsmuir toured the prairies of Alberta and Saskatchewan several times, and was able to see the slow recovery after several years of drought.

The next day's diversions, after a night in the train, included a visit to the site of dinosaur remains, a garden-party given by the Imperial Order Daughters of the Empire, and Susan's turn for a gift of juniper root wood carving. But timetables could be departed from if real need arose. The Governor-General's party reached Swift Current, a small place near Medicine Hat, on the day of the funeral of the local doctor. Since he had been much loved in the community, everyone wanted to go. The programme was quickly rearranged and the Governor-General, making no parade, slipped in with his Secretary to the back of the church, unremarked until the end of the service. And time could always be made for extra, unofficial visits, like that to an old Hutchesons' contemporary who was farming in Alsask, Saskatchewan, one of the areas worst affected by drought. This involved driving 135 miles from Medicine Hat, much of it through sand-drifts, and staying at a remarkably primitive inn. It was the experience of visiting such isolated homesteads that gave Susan the idea of starting the Prairie Libraries: the collection and distribution of books – 40,000 in two years – was the work that gave her the most satisfaction of all in her Canadian experience.

On tour, Tweedsmuir would have liked to cut out 'proconsular frills' more than he was allowed to – top hats, for instance, were *de rigueur* in every town – and he never quite realized his plan of 'touring the back parts with an ADC and picking up a lodging where I can'. But he was not going to be confined to the beaten track, geographically or socially. 'We'll take the red carpets,' he told one friend, 'because that's what people like. Then step out, leave them all behind, and talk to people.' Here his great asset was what L. S. Amery described as 'his unquenchable, all-comprehending interest in his fellow-men', which took him far beyond a general bonhomie or mateyness. He had the capacity to put himself alongside people – finding out what *their* lives were all about, what were *their* hopes and problems. 'His Excellency

The Tweedsmuirs on tour in New Brunswick.

H.E. and staff.

gets so close to people,' his Canadian ADC reported, 'he is so frightfully interested in everything that happens.' Here, being a Scot was a tremendous asset – and far beyond the obvious sense that Canada is full of Scots whose homes Tweedsmuir was likely to know. (One of the aides noted that Canada seemed to be full of people from Peebles.) In Scotland he had led no narrow sheltered life: he knew industrial Fife and Clydeside, he had been to a tough Glasgow day-school and to Glasgow University; before he left Scotland for Oxford and London and South Africa, he was at home with men and women from a wide variety of backgrounds and occupations. He himself was a man of many professions – administrator, lawyer, journalist, publisher, politician, novelist, historian. He always had a feel for the special quality of a landscape or a region, for the lives lived in it, not just at the moment of seeing, but stretching back in time; and for the loyalties of place, family, profession, trade, sport, that shape and give meaning to people's lives. It was this kind of interest that made his contacts much more than the glad-handing that public figures have to go in for.

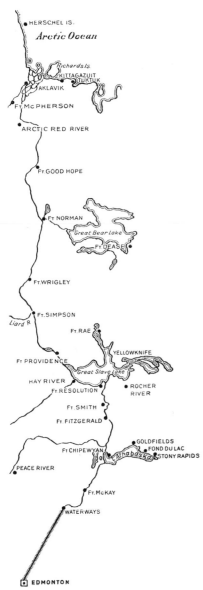

Map of the Tweedsmuirs' tour to the Arctic in 1937, showing the route through the lakes and down the Mackenzie River.

He delighted in the endless variety that he found in Canada: whether it was Gaelic-speaking miners in Nova Scotia, or old-fashioned ladies on Prince Edward Island entertaining him with songs and recitations – like a soirée at his father's church! – or the hardy Oblate Fathers of the Arctic, or the Ukrainian farmers in Saskatchewan, or the men who ran the wheat pool there – Tweedsmuir could always find some common ground. When he visited minorities – Icelanders at Gimli, Germans on the Peace River, Ukrainians at Fraserwood – he always urged them to keep their identity while accepting a new nationality, so that strands from their culture should add colour and diversity to Canadian life. This relish for diversity was one reason why he found it easy to get on with French Canadians – though he realized that the relations between Quebec and the rest of Canada were 'the most intricate of the country's problems'. As a Scot, he might have been expected to identify himself with the Scottish side of Canada; but his Scottishness worked to make him more, rather than less, sympathetic to the Frenchness of Quebec.

From the time of his arrival in Canada he had been struck by the country's provincialism. Each province tended to look at policy in terms of its own advantage, and was often astonishingly ignorant of what was happening in other provinces. The Calgary Stampede and the Dionne quintuplets would get nationwide coverage, but the successful programme of irrigation in the Prairies, for instance, was hardly known outside Saskatchewan and Alberta. So Tweedsmuir used his tours – which, with the speeches he made about them afterwards in Ottawa and Montreal and Toronto, were always well reported – to give publicity to such achievements, to tell Canadians about each other. He wanted to increase their sense of their country as a whole, to fire their imagination about its possibilities, to remind them that – for all the present economic depression – they must be expansionist, with a frontier to be pushed back.

The tour that gave Tweedsmuir most delight, and which drew most publicity – as it was meant to – was the northern journey of 1937. It was the first time that a Governor-General had gone to the Arctic. He was going because the North was all-important to Canada, and most Canadians knew nothing about it. Splendid work had been done by miners and engineers and agriculturalists, by doctors and nurses and teachers and men who flew small aircraft, to push the habitable frontier farther north and develop its resources. Little of this had been publicized – in contrast to all that had been written, and shown in photographs and films, of the similar Russian developments in northern Siberia. By this journey Tweedsmuir was challenging Canadians to discard the picture of a barren North inimical to man. The North could help to counter Canadian provincialism, for 'It makes a link with all Canada, for the North is a common interest.'

A picture, taken by Shuldham Redfern, which records a visit to Grey Owl, the writer who passed as an Indian (which he was not) and whose books on wild life Tweedsmuir admired. He is seen chatting up one of Grey Owl's friends, and being photographed by his ADC John Boyle; Grey Owl is begging them to stay till the beavers come for their evening feed, and the pilot is worried about getting back to Edmonton in daylight.

The vessel which took the Governor-General's party 1,300 miles down the Slave River and the Mackenzie River to the Arctic.

Opposite: The inhabitants of a Hudson's Bay Company's post on the Mackenzie River turn out to see the Governor-General, the first to come so far north.

The tour started at Edmonton in Alberta: the party went by train to Waterways, the base depot for the Hudson's Bay Company's stores; and were taken to the Abasand oilfields, 'where they say that by extracting oil from sand, there will be enough oil to supply the world for a hundred years'. They then embarked on one of the company's regular river-service boats, a stern-wheeler that seemed a cross between a Nile steamer and a Henley houseboat, and chugged peacefully between the wooded banks of the Athabasca River to Lake Athabasca and Fort Fitzgerald. To avoid the rapids on the Slave River they took an ancient car for sixteen bumpy miles to Fort Smith, then back to the river and another Hudson Bay stern-wheeler, the *Distributor*, for the ten-day voyage down the Slave River and the Mackenzie River to a twisty course through the vast quagmire of the delta, and so to Aklavik. They called in at every Hudson Bay post – most of them small settlements with a trading depot, a police station, a few dwellings and sometimes a

Journey's end for the trip Down North: Aklavik on the Mackenzie River delta, the centre for the fur posts along the Arctic shore and offshore islands.

church — and were welcomed by friendly Indians, Mounties, traders, nuns, priests, oilmen and rather fierce dogs. At Aklavik the reception committee was headed by 'Archibald the Arctic', as Bishop Fleming liked to sign himself.

Tweedsmuir enjoyed the voyage hugely — the changing scene of wood and crag, tundra and swamp; the peaceful hours of sailing and the cheerful encounters ashore. Aklavik, in the middle of the delta, was a disappointment — a mess of a town, though marvellous work was being done there by priests, doctors and nurses. Much cleaner and healthier was Tuktu Yaktu on the open shore, the most northerly settlement on the mainland, to which Tweedsmuir flew in a Canadian Air Force plane. His return journey south was by air, with detours to visit Eskimos in Coronation Gulf, to see the pitchblende mine at the Great Bear Lake and the gold workings at Yellowknife, and to fish and stalk caribou on the Barrens. He came back from his tour, 2,000 miles by water, 3,000 by air, extolling the North: where winter was kindlier than in the plains; where summer, with its double allowance of sunshine, was beautiful and bountiful; where every year the limits of cultivation were pushed back, where there was untold mineral wealth to be extracted. It was 'a new world, held together by the cheapest, safest air travel in existence'.

The tour was widely reported, in Britain and the United States as well as Canada, and the North was brought further into the urban Canadian's consciousness. The reports also made clear the zest and enthusiasm of the Governor-General. Here is one picture of him, from Margaret Bourke-White, the photographer, who accompanied the party. He is sitting on the deck of the stern-wheeler *Athabasca River*, making the index for his book on the Emperor Augustus:

A long narrow table had been contrived for him with a couple of planks, and there he sat with the fluttering little white paper markers of his index all over the place. Our cargo almost swallowed him up. His spare form was all but lost in the midst of the pig crates, the cage of chickens, the tractor, the assortment of agricultural implements which surrounded him.

Another picture comes from himself, describing to his old friend and climbing partner Stair Gillon how temptation came to him at Fort Norman with the sight of Bear Mountain rearing up 1,300 feet above the Mackenzie. The face had never been climbed, and up he had to go:

The rock was rotten and slanting the wrong way but I took it cautiously and had no difficulties except at the very top where there is an overhang. I managed to drag up an Indian so that he could give me a back, and wriggled my way up.

Tweedsmuir, that old hand on the Coolins and Dolomites, was elated – all the more so because 'the rest of my staff, including an inspector of police, got stuck on the lower rocks and had to be rescued by ropes!'

On the return journey by air from the Arctic, in a single-engined plane of the Royal Canadian Air Force, Tweedsmuir stopped at the Eldorado pitchblende mine at Great Bear Lake, then the world's chief producer of radium.

The zest which sent a sixty-year-old public man scrambling up Bear Mountain, which had made him take up skiing at an age when most skiers are thinking of giving it up, was one of the most valuable qualities he brought to his office. Only later did he realize that the Arctic tour, though he did not feel it at the time, 'was really too heavy a job for a man of my age, and the unconscious fatigue went straight to my digestion'.

At this point I should like to make a confession. When I started work on my full-length biography of John Buchan (published in 1965), my notion of his years in Canada was that he had been given the Governor-Generalship as a sort of consolation prize for lack of success in British politics, for never having been in the Government; and that it was an ornamental job, a sinecure, an anti-climax to an active life. Many of his friends had thought the same at the time of his appointment. But the moment that I went to work, read his letters from Canada, went to Canada myself and talked to Canadians, I realized that this was the job of his life which, more than any other he had held, allowed him to make full use of his diverse talents. Tweedsmuir gave much to Canada because Canada gave so much to him: a sense of purpose and a sense of adventure, of belief in possibilities, the chance of the unforeseen, of something challenging round the corner – the sense that is so strong in John Buchan's stories and gives them their continuing appeal. And Canada gave him – through his journey to the Arctic, his flights over the Barrens, his sight of the unexplored regions of the Nahanni River – the inspiration and the setting for his last novel, *Sick Heart River*, where he transcends the limit of the adventure story and writes his own testament.

After finishing his biography of Augustus, he had started on his memoirs. *Memory Hold-the-Door* (in America, *Pilgrim's Way*) was, he told a correspondent, 'not an ordinary autobiography or any attempt to tell the story of my life – but rather an attempt to pick out certain highlights and expound the impressions made upon me at different stages – Oxford, the Bar, South Africa, Parliament etc'. The tone is that of the man of affairs looking back to his beginnings – there is a beautiful evocation of the Border country – remembering his friends and musing on the changes he has seen in his life. He recalls his early efforts to teach himself to write, his apprenticeship to Pater and Stevenson; but on his later writings there are only seven rather dismissive pages, as if his success as a man of letters had been something of a happy accident, a pleasant addition to his public career. Whether, as a writer, he had come up to his early ambitions, he does not say.

There is little introspection in *Memory Hold-the-Door*, no wondering whether he might have achieved more had he not aimed at so many targets. But in *Sick Heart River*, the novel that he started in 1939, he

Over the Coast Range to Bella Coola, after ten days camping and trekking in the newly named Tweedsmuir Park in British Columbia. On such flights across the mountains Tweedsmuir was always trying to spot any hidden sanctuary of wood and meadow in the tangle of hills below: such a place as he was to make the object of Leithen's quest in *Sick Heart River*.

Tweedsmuir signed Canada's declaration of war on Germany on 7 September 1939; soon afterwards, Canadian troops were on their way to Britain.

looked more closely at himself — though at one remove. Its hero is Sir Edward Leithen, the lawyer and politician who had figured in many of the thrillers. Now Buchan was making Leithen more and more like himself in his body, his character and his experience. (This struck his secretary strongly as she took down the story which he dictated from his own scribbled manuscript.) Leithen, told he is fatally ill, goes off on a quixotic quest to rescue a man lost in the Canadian North. He spends much time looking back at his life and wondering what it all amounted to. He had enjoyed it, but in the light of his impending death, and in the perspective of the northern waste, his successes as barrister and Cabinet minister now seem trivial. He has been too immersed in the world's bustle, too deceived by its glitter.

Buchan was not given to brooding over the might-have-beens of life — he left that to his mother. But I think that through Leithen he was expressing real regret that his days had been so filled with bustle — committees, lectures, meetings, journalism, giving all manner of worthy causes a helping hand — that there had been too little time to take his bearings, to meditate, from time to time to take life easy. He had driven himself too hard.

He had begun *Sick Heart River* in the autumn of 1939, at a sad time. In September he had signed Canada's declaration of war against Germany. 'This is the third war I have been in,' he wrote to an old friend, 'and no-one could hate the horrible thing more than I do.' His three sons were in uniform, and would be at risk – Johnnie and Alastair with Canadian regiments, Billy with the R.A.F. Instead of the journeys he loved, his days were filled with reviewing troops, visiting convoys, and appealing for war charities. And his duodenal ulcer had once more got the better of him. During a cure at Ruthin Castle, North Wales, when he was home on leave in 1938, he had put on a stone in weight, but now he had lost it all and was down to under nine stone. He had been offered a second five-year term as Governor-General, but knew he would not have the strength for it. So it would soon be goodbye to Canada, and by now this would be a hard uprooting. 'Leaving Canada,' he told his sister, 'is going to be like pulling up mandrakes.'

In the end he did not have to face it. Early in February 1940 he had a cerebral thrombosis, and he died a week later, without regaining consciousness. In the story he had so recently completed Leithen had been made to die at Easter 1940 – only a few weeks after the death of his inventor.

From his boyhood John Buchan had set himself a strenuous course, and he had attained many of his goals. Most of the items on those lists of Things to be Done had been ticked off. He had succeeded as public man, as story-teller, as historian. But what in that early poem he had wished for himself at the twilight stage, as coda to an active life, he was denied. For him there was no 'happy moorland peace' at the close of the day.

Outside Rideau Hall, February 1939.

Overleaf: Buchan's grave in the churchyard at Elsfield: the circular stone was designed by Sir Herbert Baker. The cypresses are now well grown.

1875 John, eldest son of the Rev. John Buchan and Helen Buchan (née Masterton), born 26 August at 20 York Place, Perth; father minister of the Knox Church (Free Church).

1876– Family moves to Pathhead, Fife,
88 on father's appointment to Free Church; John attends Board School, then burgh school and High School at Kirkcaldy. Holidays with Masterton grandparents at Broughton Green, Peeblesshire. Anna Buchan born 1877; William 1880; Walter 1883; Violet 1888 (d. 1893).

1888 Rev. John Buchan called to John Knox Free Church in the Gorbals, Glasgow. Family lives at 34 Queen Mary Avenue. John attends Hutchesons' Grammar School.

1892 Wins bursary to Glasgow University; enrols for general MA course.

1894 Edits *Essays and Apothegms of Francis Lord Bacon.* Alastair Buchan born.

1895 Wins classical scholarship to Brasenose College, Oxford.

1895– While at Oxford publishes *Sir*
99 *Quixote of the Moors, Scholar-Gipsies, John Burnet of Barns, Brasenose College, Grey Weather*; contributes to the *Yellow Book*; reads mss for John Lane. Elected President of the Union; takes First Class in Literae Humaniores (Greats).

1899 Takes rooms in the Temple and reads for the Bar. Writes regularly for the *Spectator*; publishes *A Lost Lady of Old Years* and *The Half-Hearted.*

1901 Invited by Milner, High Commissioner for South Africa, to join his staff; in September sails for Cape Town.

1901– Shares a house near Johannesburg
03 with three Oxford friends; works on refugee camps, land settlement, and administration of the new colonies of Orange River and Transvaal. Travels in Transvaal and Swaziland.

1903– Back in London, works as a
06 barrister specializing in tax cases; writes for the *Spectator*. Climbing holidays with Anna in Skye and Chamonix. *The African Colony; The Law Relating to the Taxation of*

Foreign Income; A Lodge in the Wilderness.

1906 In December, accepts offer to join Nelson's, publishers, as chief literary adviser; is engaged to Susan Grosvenor.

1907 Works at Nelson's in Edinburgh from January to June. On 15 July marries Susan Grosvenor at St George's, Hanover Square, London. Honeymoon in Hampshire, Dolomites and Venice. Takes house at 40 Hyde Park Square. Works at Nelson's London office, with monthly trips to Edinburgh.

1908 Alice Buchan born 5 June.

1910 Moves to 13 Bryanston Street. Rev. John and Mrs Buchan retire from Glasgow to Peebles. Buchans go on spring cruise to the Aegean. *Prester John.*

1911 Buchan adopted as Unionist candidate for Peeblesshire and Selkirk. Rev. John Buchan dies on 19 November. John Norman Stuart Buchan born 25 November.

1912 Fishing holiday in Norway in June. Buchans move to 76 Portland Place. William Buchan, home on leave from India, dies in November. First sign of Buchan's trouble which led to duodenal ulcer. *The Moon Endureth.*

1913 *The Marquis of Montrose; The Power-House* (in *Blackwood's Magazine*).

1914 In August, Buchan ordered to rest; in bed at Broadstairs begins *The Thirty-Nine Steps*; suggests

that Nelson's should publish a history of the war in serial parts.

1915 Works on Nelson's *History of the War*; lectures on the course of the war; visits British Expeditionary Force in France and Flanders as correspondent for *The Times*; becomes a director of Nelson's. *The Thirty-Nine Steps.*

1916 William Buchan born 10 January. Buchan gazetted Major in Intelligence Corps (later Lt-Col.); visits GHQ in France, and Grand Fleet at Scapa Flow. *Greenmantle.*

1917 In February, has operation for duodenal ulcer. Appointed Director of Information, responsible to Prime Minister. Alastair Buchan (brother) dies of wounds.

1918 Becomes Director of Intelligence in new Ministry of Information, where Beaverbrook is Minister. Alastair Buchan born 9 September.

1919 Buys Elsfield Manor, near Oxford; appointed a director of Reuters. *Mr Standfast.*

1920– Lives at Elsfield, travelling daily to
26 London on Nelson and Reuter business. Holidays in the Highlands and Shetland; in 1924 visits the United States and Canada. *The Path of the King; Huntingtower; Midwinter; The Three Hostages; John Macnab; The Dancing Floor.*

1927 Elected to Parliament as Member for the Scottish universities. *Witch Wood.*

1928 *Montrose.*

1929 At general election, heads the poll for Scottish universities. Resigns from Nelson's. *The Courts of the Morning*.

1930 *Castle Gay*.

1931 At general election returned unopposed for Scottish universities. *The Blanket of the Dark*.

1932 Created Companion of Honour. Holiday in Faeroes. *Sir Walter Scott; The Gap in the Curtain*.

1933 Appointed High Commissioner to the General Assembly of the Church of Scotland. Resides at Holyrood with his family for the ten days of the Assembly. *A Prince of the Captivity*.

1934 Again High Commissioner. Honorary DCL from Oxford University; Honorary Fellow of Brasenose College. Visits New York to give dedicatory address at opening of Butler Library, Columbia University. *Oliver Cromwell; The Free Fishers*.

1935 Appointed Governor-General of Canada; created Baron Tweedsmuir; given freedom of Edinburgh. In November the Tweedsmuirs arrive in Canada and settle into Rideau Hall, official residence in Ottawa. *The House of the Four Winds*.

1936 Tours western Ontario Prairies and British Columbia. In July, entertains President Roosevelt at the Citadel, Quebec. Visit from Mrs Buchan and Anna. *The Island of Sheep*.

1937 In April, visits Washington as guest of President Roosevelt; trips to Maritimes, the Arctic, Tweedsmuir Park in British Columbia. Elected Chancellor of Edinburgh University. Mrs Buchan dies. *Augustus*.

1938 Tours drought areas of Prairies. In June receives honorary degrees at Harvard and Yale; sails for Britain; installed as Chancellor of Edinburgh University; goes for two months to clinic at Ruthin; returns to Canada in October.

1939 Tours British Columbia and Hudson Bay. In May, King George VI and Queen Elizabeth visit Canada. On 9 September signs Canada's declaration of war against Germany. In November goes to New York for medical treatment.

1940 Suffers cerebral thrombosis on 6 February; dies on the 11th. Funeral in Ottawa; ashes taken home for burial at Elsfield. *Memory Hold-the-Door*.

BIBLIOGRAPHY

Some books about Buchan and his family:

Anna Buchan (O. Douglas) *Unforgettable, Unforgotten* (1945)
——*Farewell to Priorsford* (1950), a book by and about Anna Buchan
Two of her novels, based on the Buchan family life:
——*The Setons* (1917)
——*Eliza for Common* (1928)
Lord Tweedsmuir (Johnnie Buchan) *Hudson's Bay Trader* (1951)
——*Always a Countryman* (1935)
Susan Tweedsmuir *John Buchan by his Wife and Friends* (1947). Includes contributions from Charles Dick, Roger Merriman, Violet Markham, Sir Roderick Jones, Lord Macmillan, Lord Baldwin, Walter Elliot, Catherine Carswell, A.L. Rowse, Janet Adam Smith, Leonard Brockington, Sir Shuldham Redfern, Alastair Buchan
——*Carnets Canadiens* (1938)
——*The Lilac and the Rose* (1952)
——*A Winter Bouquet* (1954)
——*The Edwardian Lady* (1966)
S.A. Gillon Article on Buchan in *Dictionary of National Biography, 1931–40*
Janet Adam Smith *John Buchan* (1965)

There are passages about Buchan in the following autobiographies and memoirs:

Arnold Bennett *Journals* vol. II (1931); vol. III (1933)
Ferris Greenslet *Under the Bridge* (1943)
H. Hensley Henson *Retrospect of an Unimportant Life* Vol. II (1943); vol. III (1950)
Sir Roderick Jones *A Life in Reuters* (1951)
Tom Jones *Welsh Broth* (1951)
David Garnett (ed.) *Letters of T.E. Lawrence* (1938)
A.W. Lawrence (ed.) *Letters to T.E. Lawrence* (1962)
Gilbert Murray *An Unfinished Autobiography* (1960)
——Preface to *The Clearing House,* a selection from the writings of John Buchan (1946)
M. Newbolt *Later Life and Letters of Sir Henry Newbolt* (1942)
Lina Waterfield *A Castle in Italy* (1961)

Critical writings on Buchan and his work:

David Daniell *The Interpreter's House* (1975)

and essays in the following collections:

Graham Greene *The Lost Childhood* (1950)
C.M. Grieve (Hugh MacDiarmid) *Contemporary Studies* (1926)
Gertrude Himmelfarb *Victorian Minds* (1968)

'Janitor' (Mary Lyttelton and J.G. Lockhart) *The Feet of the Young Men* (1928)

Violet Markham *Friendship's Harvest* (1956)

John Raymond *England's on the Anvil* (1958)

M.R. Ridley *Second Thoughts* (1965)

Richard Usborne *Clubland Heroes* (1953)

JOHN BUCHAN'S WRITINGS

(The American title, where it differs from the British, is given in square brackets)

1894 *Essays and Apothegms of Francis Lord Bacon* (edited with introduction)
1895 *Sir Quixote of the Moors*
1896 *Scholar-Gipsies*: essays
1898 *John Burnet of Barns*
Brasenose College
1899 *Grey Weather*: stories and poems
A Lost Lady of Old Years
1900 *The Half-Hearted*
1902 *The Watcher by the Threshold*: five stories, including 'No-Man's-Land' and 'The Watcher by the Threshold'
1903 *The African Colony*
1905 *The Law Relating to the Taxation of Foreign Income*
1906 *A Lodge in the Wilderness*
1908 *Some Eighteenth Century byways*: essays and articles
1910 *Prester John* [*The Great Diamond Pipe*]
1912 *The Moon Endureth*: stories and poems
1913 *The Marquis of Montrose*
Andrew Jameson, Lord Ardwall
1915–19 Nelson's *History of the War*
1915 *The Thirty-Nine Steps*
Salute to Adventurers
1916 *The Power-House*
Greenmantle
1917 *Poems, Scots and English*
1919 *Mr Standfast*

These for Remembrance: memoirs of friends killed in the war
The Island of Sheep 'by Cadmus and Harmonia' (with Susan Buchan)
1920 *The History of the South African Forces in France*
Francis and Riversdale Grenfell
1921 *The Path of the King*
1921–22 *A History of the Great War*
1922 *Huntingtower*
A Book of Escapes and Hurried Journeys
1923 *The Last Secrets*: essays and articles on remote and unexplored places
Midwinter
1924 *The Three Hostages*
Lord Minto
The Northern Muse (compiled)
1925 *The History of the Royal Scots Fusiliers*
John Macnab
1926 *The Dancing Floor*
Homilies and Recreations: essays and addresses
1927 *Witch Wood*
1928 *The Runagates Club*: stories
Montrose
1929 *The Courts of the Morning*
The Causal and the Casual in History (Rede Lecture)
1930 *The Kirk in Scotland* (with George Adam Smith)
Castle Gay
1931 *The Blanket of the Dark*
The Novel and the Fairy Tale
1932 *Sir Walter Scott*
The Gap in the Curtain
Julius Caesar
The Magic Walking-Stick
1933 *The Massacre of Glencoe*
A Prince of the Captivity
1934 *The Free Fishers*
Gordon at Khartoum
Oliver Cromwell
1935 *The King's Grace*
The House of the Four Winds
1936 *The Island of Sheep* [*The Man from the Norlands*]
1937 *Augustus*

1940 *Memory Hold-the-Door* [*Pilgrim's Way*]
Comments and Characters: selections from Buchan's contributions to the *Scottish Review*
Canadian Occasions: addresses
1941 *Sick Heart River* [*Mountain Meadow*]

The Long Traverse [*Lake of Gold*]

The next works that Buchan planned were a novel, *The Island Called Lone,* and a book about fishing of which he completed two chapters (printed at the end of *Memory Hold-the-Door*) with the pencilled title *Pilgrim's Rest.*

All illustrations connected with the family and not otherwise attributed are gratefully acknowledged to John Buchan's surviving children, Lady Fairfax-Lucy, Lord Tweedsmuir and the Hon. William Buchan.

Frontispiece: John Buchan, 1906.

Page numbers in italics refer to illustrations.
Buchan's writings are indexed under the entry for Buchan himself.